T0020864

A SHORT
HISTORY
of the
WORLD *in*
50 BOOKS

Some other bestselling titles by Daniel Smith

How to Think Like a Philosopher

*How to Think Like Sherlock: Improve Your Powers of
Observation, Memory and Deduction*

*The Ardlamont Mystery: The Real-Life Story Behind the
Creation of Sherlock Holmes*

*The Little Book of Big Ideas: 150 Concepts and
Breakthroughs that Transformed History*

Think You Know it All? The Activity Book for Grown-Ups

A SHORT HISTORY
of the
WORLD *in*
50 BOOKS

Daniel Smith

Michael O'Mara Books Limited

First published in Great Britain in 2022 by
Michael O'Mara Books Limited
9 Lion Yard
Tremadoc Road
London SW4 7NQ

A CIP catalogue record for this book is available from the British Library

Papers used by Michael O'Mara Books Limited are natural, recyclable
products made from wood grown in sustainable forests. The manufacturing
processes conform to the environmental regulations of the country of
origin.

ISBN: 978-1-78929-408-8 in hardback print format
ISBN: 978-1-78929-478-1 in trade paperback format
ISBN: 978-1-78929-411-8 in ebook format

2 3 4 5 6 7 8 9 10

Designed and typeset by Claire Cater
Illustrations by Aubrey Smith, map by David Woodroffe
Printed and bound by CPI Group (UK) Ltd, Croydon, CR0 4YY
www.mombooks.com

For Charlotte and Ben –
my brilliant bookworms

CONTENTS

CONTENTS

Part II: The Middle Ages

Part III: The Early Modern Age

INTRODUCTION

*'In books lies the soul of the whole Past Time;
the articulate audible voice of the Past,
when the body and material substance of it
has altogether vanished like a dream.'*

Thomas Carlyle, 'The Hero as a Man of Letters' (1841)

What is a book? Technically, we might say it is any set of printed pages that are fastened together inside a cover. But what, then, of all those books that you can read on your electronic device? And how do we account for those ancient texts perhaps inscribed on a stone tablet or even the bones of a sacrificial animal? We have a rich literary history that far pre-dates the technology that gave us paper, let alone the wherewithal to bind that paper together and stick a cover on it. Better, then, to adopt a much broader definition – the book is a written work of fiction or non-fiction created with the intention that it should be read by others. On what material it was originally set down hardly matters.

We are the only species, of course, to produce books: an object that encapsulates the ideas and imagination of its author or authors. The book has a unique status as an emblem of human culture and civilization. It is a vessel for sharing stories, dispersing knowledge, examining the nature of our extraordinary species and imagining what lies beyond our known world. As Carlyle suggests, books ultimately provide an invaluable and comprehensive record of what it means to be human. Sometimes, they may even give us a window onto the divine. As Jorge Luis Borges once wrote: 'I have always imagined Paradise as a kind of library.'

This volume takes a curated list of fifty of the most influential books of all time, putting each into its historical context. From ancient game-changers like the *Epic of Gilgamesh* and the *Iliad*, through sacred texts and works of philosophical rumination by the likes of Confucius and Plato, via scientific treatises, historic 'firsts' (such as the first printed book) and cultural works of enduring impact (think Shakespeare, Cervantes and Joseph Heller, these are volumes that are at once both products of their societies and vital texts in moulding those same civilizations.

What this selection isn't is a celebration of the literary canon, a reaffirmation of the 'best' books from the past. You will find no Austen or Dickens here, nor Melville or Dostoyevsky or García Márquez. There is Shakespeare and Cervantes and Tolstoy, but not because they are somehow 'better' than those others. Rather, this collection aims to select books that reflect the passage of human history – mostly our progress and occasionally our regression too. Most not only reflect, though, but themselves changed how we think and live – not merely symbols of history but agents of it. By definition, they are 'important' works and, in broad critical terms, 'great' works too. But this book is not concerned with which works are the greatest of all – there are plenty of other volumes that try to figure that out, and good luck to them.

Inevitably, making a selection such as this is highly subjective. It is a process as much defined by omission as by what is chosen. In selecting fifty titles, we can only hope to dip our toe (our little toe at that) into the vast pool of literature from ages gone by. In doing so, it is folly to make any claim for definitiveness. Instead, we are playing a literary game. Which of the fifty choices are indisputable? Which are taking a place better deserved by some other work? Everyone will have their own ideas. In the end, it matters little that we all agree. More important is that by turning our minds to the question in the first place, we might meet some unfamiliar works, revisit some old favourites, and gain some insight and pleasure in the process.

Books are brilliant. They are building blocks of our collective identity. They are monuments to our civilization. They are gateways to new worlds. We cannot explore them enough. Carl Sagan summed it up elegantly: 'Across the millennia, an author is speaking clearly and silently inside your head, directly to you. Writing is perhaps the greatest of human inventions, binding together people who never knew each other, citizens of distant epochs. Books break the shackles of time. A book is proof that humans are capable of working magic.'

I

THE ANCIENT WORLD

TITLE: *THE EPIC OF GILGAMESH*

AUTHOR: UNKNOWN
DATE: THIRD MILLENNIUM BC

. . . .

Widely considered the world's first known work of literary fiction, *The Epic of Gilgamesh* is a long poem telling the adventures of Gilgamesh, a king from the ancient Sumerian civilization centred around the modern-day region of Iraq and Syria. (Historical records suggest that there was indeed a king by that name who probably ruled in the early part of the third millennium BC.) Today, we have some 3,200 lines of the text, thought to be about 80–90 per cent of the original total. Authored in the latter part of the third millennium BC, *Gilgamesh* may justly be regarded as the first great leap forward in literary history – the original masterwork of imaginative thinking preserved in written form.

The story itself is quite the romp. Gilgamesh, described as one-third human and two-thirds deity (his mother, Ninsun, being a goddess and his father, a mere mortal), is King of Uruk, a sparkling walled city in southern Mesopotamia. Ginormous and strong, he is also rather wayward, lording it over the men of Uruk with his athletic prowess and exercising what he considers to be his right to engage with the city's women, especially new brides. The citizens grow tired of his misconduct and complain to the gods, so the goddess Aruru fashions him a companion, a fellow giant called Enkidu, from a piece of clay. Enkidu, it is hoped, will keep him on the straight and narrow.

Enkidu is animalistic in nature, although imbued with human intelligence too. However, after he is tempted to engage in a prolonged sexual dalliance with a human (a temple prostitute called Shamhat; intercourse is said to have lasted for an entire week, or even two according to some interpretations), Enkidu is rejected by the animals and becomes fully human. He is effectively cast out of his old world and propelled into a new, often more complicated, one. His new morality causes him to challenge Gilgamesh on his behaviour and the pair wrestle in a ferocious contest. But at its end, they enter into a friendship that sends them on various adventures.

Some while after their battle, the duo go to the Forest of Cedar, where they scheme to take some of its sacred trees after killing their feared protector, a monster called Humbaba the Terrible. Later on, the goddess Ishtar expresses her desire for Gilgamesh but he rejects her, prompting the scorned goddess to send the 'Bull of Heaven' to take terrible vengeance on him if he continues to spurn her. But Gilgamesh and Enkidu succeed in slaying the beast. The deaths of Humbaba and the Bull inspire the wrath of the gods, who punish Enkidu with a long, drawn-out death over twelve bed-ridden days of illness.

Devastated by the loss of his friend and determined to escape a similar fate, Gilgamesh then seeks to learn the secret of eternal life from the only human survivors of a Great Flood. To reach them, he must undertake a long and dangerous journey. But it is to no avail, since he learns that death is unavoidable. Gilgamesh himself is dead, probably of old age (although it is not explicitly stated) before the story ends, the citizens of Uruk mourning the passing of their ruler.

Gilgamesh includes many of the tropes that became staples of classical heroic epics, perhaps most clearly serving as a template for Homer's *Iliad* (not least the echoes of Enkidu in the character of Patroclus) and *Odyssey*. Many scholars also argue that *Gilgamesh* shares some common ground with the Bible.

The story of Enkidu – a man created divinely from the soil – and his 'expulsion' from his natural home after being 'tempted' by a woman (Shamhat) has obvious parallels with the story of Adam and Eve and their fall from Eden. But perhaps even more striking is Gilgamesh's visit to Utnapishtim and his wife in pursuit of the secret to eternal life. In that episode, Utnapishtim relates how the god Enlil brought down a great flood upon the world as punishment for man's failings. However, Utnapishtim was forewarned by another god, who told him to prepare a boat that could carry him, his family and the seeds of all living things to safety. When the flood comes, only those on board the vessel are saved among all humankind. Their boat is eventually grounded on the top of a mountain, at which point Utnapishtim released a series of birds (including a dove) to seek dry land. Save for a few name changes, it is an almost identical narrative to that of Noah and his ark as related in the biblical book of Genesis. Whether *Gilgamesh* was itself a source for the Noah story or both stories simply reflect a shared storytelling tradition is uncertain.

The literary history of *Gilgamesh* is almost as fascinating as the story the epic tells. Originally a series of Sumerian poems written in cuneiform script around 2100 BC, the fuller version that we know today comes from the Babylonians, who inscribed it in the Akkadian language on twelve stone tablets around 1200–1000 BC. But after about 600 BC, *Gilgamesh* became a largely lost classic. Then, in the 1850s, a large number of inscribed tablets were discovered by a British-led team of archaeologists on the site of an ancient library in Nineveh, close to modern-day Mosul in Iraq. The relics were duly sent to the British Museum. After several years, the museum called upon a volunteer – a banknote engraver called George Smith, who had left school when aged just fourteen (although already imbued with a fascination for Assyrian history and culture) – to help analyse the shards that had been sitting uninvestigated in a storeroom. Over ten years or so in the

1860s and 1870s he succeeded in translating a number of them and so reintroduced the epic back to the world. There was a certain elegant poetry in an eager amateur, as opposed to some noted man of letters, reconnecting the world with its first great work of literature.

BY GEORGE!

Quite whether George Smith fully realized the extent of his achievement is uncertain, given that he died on a study trip to Aleppo in 1876, aged just thirty-six. Much of his own excitement around the fragments that he decoded centres on his belief that they confirmed the truth of Genesis. When he read of a Great Flood that put paid to humankind save for one man and his family, he is said to have jumped out of his chair in glee and run elatedly around his room at the museum. When he addressed the Society of Biblical Archaeology on his discovery, the prime minister, William Gladstone, was in the audience and Smith's discoveries made headlines across the globe.

TITLE: *TAO TE CHING*

AUTHOR: LAOZI (ATTRIBUTED TO)
DATE: FIRST MILLENNIUM BC

. . . .

The *Tao Te Ching* (which loosely translates as *The Way and Its Power*) is the chief spiritual guide for followers of the ancient Chinese philosophy of Taoism. Taoists advocate leading a simple, humble and pious life, and in so doing achieving balance with the Tao (which effectively equates to the universe in its material and spiritual manifestations). In simplistic terms, adherents seek a peaceful existence at one with nature, expounding such concepts as virtue (*de*), naturalness (*ziran*) and non-action (*wuwei*).

The book's purported author, Laozi, is a highly disputed figure, who may have lived around the sixth century BC as a contemporary of Confucius, but who some scholars have suggested was instead alive at a later point sometime in the next two centuries. Many others doubt whether Laozi (often translated as 'Old Master') was a real person at all. Instead, there is a large school of thought that thinks the *Tao Te Ching* is a collection of poetry and sayings originating from a number of different authors.

The volume aims to provide guidance to Taoists as to how they can exist in harmony with the universe. Although Taoism allows for deities, the universal energy at the core of its philosophy is not regarded in terms of a godhead. Rather, this energy connects everything, creating a unified whole, and adherents attempt to live in balance with its oppositional forces – for example, light and dark, fire and water, action and inaction. These dualities are encapsulated in the concept of *yin* and *yang*.

The text of the *Tao Te Ching* is relatively short, comprising just over eighty short sections and only around five thousand Chinese characters. At its heart are the 'three Jewels' of compassion, humility and moderation. Its various teachings, often summarized in a few short words, are frequently mystical and hard to pin down. In particular, the concept of *wuwei* has inspired many interpretations, although most agree that it promotes the avoidance of damaging intervention rather than passive inaction for its own sake: 'Do nothing and everything is done.' In a world where the impetus is towards perpetual motion and non-ending action, such an argument represents at the very least a challenge to the accepted orthodoxy, if not an outright threat. Furthermore, its implicit criticism of the excesses of a ruling class who oversaw an almost constant state of flux and disharmony renders the *Tao Te Ching* a much more radical and confrontational text than it might first appear. Consider the barbed nature of its observation: 'When the Master governs, the people are hardly aware that he exists.'

The first significant reference to Laozi being its author is found in the writings of second- to first-century-BC historian Sima Qian. It has been suggested Laozi may have been a historian himself or that he perhaps worked at the imperial archives. Other later narratives claimed that he had lived for hundreds of years and was the latest in a long line of reincarnations. But in truth, it is hard to discern a genuine biographical figure. Hence increasing support for the idea of the *Tao Te Ching* as being an anthology. It is thought that the work might have been brought together, edited and refined over perhaps centuries in the latter half of the first millennium BC.

A series of bamboo tablets were discovered in a tomb in the province of Hubei in central China in 1993 that included several parts in common with the *Tao Te Ching*. Dating from no more recently than 300 BC, these are the oldest-known extant examples of *Tao Te Ching* text. Other later examples of the book and commentaries based upon it have been found inscribed variously on bamboo, silk and paper. The use of the title *Tao Te Ching* emerged during the rule of the Han dynasty, which lasted from 202 BC to AD 220. Taoism served as a significant strain of philosophy in Chinese life across the ensuing centuries, competing for space alongside the not entirely unrelated Buddhist belief system, as well as Confucianism and Legalism (which called for strong government rooted in a system of law and order). Even when these philosophical schools seemed at odds with one another, Taoism regularly provided the terms of reference through which their differences could be reconciled.

Taoism blossomed under the Tang dynasty (AD 618–907), with the Tang emperors even claiming Laozi as their ancestor. It would remain a major feature of China's spiritual landscape for the best part of the next thousand years, although its influence declined from the seventeenth century onwards, particularly in relation to the ongoing influence of Buddhism and Confucianism. It was only in the following century that it significantly entered into the Western consciousness, when it was translated into Latin by Jesuit priests. The first English translation only appeared in 1868.

ZHUANGZI

The other great work of Taoism is *Zhuangzi*, named after its author who lived in the fourth century BC. Also sometimes referred to as *Nanhua zhenjing* (*The Pure Classic of Nanhua*), the collection of anecdotes and fables draws heavily on the *Tao Te Ching* but is regarded by many critics as exploring its Taoist credo in greater depth. Its author's character permeates the text and we discover a man who wears old shoes held together with string because the material world matters not to him, who cannot mourn the loss of his wife because her passing is but an expression of the natural way, and who himself declines a coffin for his funeral and cares not whether it is the birds above ground or the worms below it who should feast upon his dead body.

Its death knell seemed to come in the 1950s when the Chinese authorities implemented a ban on formal religion, yet still Taoism has maintained a foothold within the country and more broadly internationally. Today, it can boast adherents in the millions. Its message of seeking to live in harmony with the natural world, so elegantly espoused, is one that resonates now perhaps more than ever before as we come to terms with the effects of the damage our species has wrought on our planet. 'Love the world as yourself; then you can care for all things,' runs one of its verses. How thoroughly modern and timeless.

TITLE: *ILIAD*

AUTHOR: HOMER
DATE: *C.* **EIGHTH/SEVENTH CENTURY BC**

. . . .

The *Iliad* is an epic poem of the Ancient Greek world, spanning 15,693 lines and 24 books to tell the story of the Trojan War, fought between the city of Troy and its Greek enemies. In common with other works of antiquity, there is academic debate as to the precise nature of its authorship, although it is widely attributed to Homer, who is also credited with writing the *Odyssey* – by common consent the two works upon which Ancient Greek literature took root and blossomed, and that have proved an enduring influence on the entirety of Western culture.

The *Iliad* is set amid the last year of the ten-year siege of Troy by Achaean (i.e. Greek) forces, a situation precipitated by Paris, a prince of Troy, kidnapping Helen, the wife of Menelaus, king of the Greek city-state of Sparta. (Helen's detention led to the launch of a vast fleet to save her, prompting Christopher Marlowe many centuries later to consider her beauty with the question: 'Was this the face that launch'd a thousand ships?') The action takes place at the tail-end of the Bronze Age, around 1200 BC – some four hundred years before Homer is said to have written the poem. The historical authenticity of the saga is a moot subject. For a long time, Troy itself was regarded as a fictional creation, although archaeological evidence turned up in the nineteenth century suggests it was likely a real city located in modern-day Turkey. But whether Homer's saga of war reflects a genuine conflict or is rather the product of his imagination, or perhaps a synthesis of several genuine historical events and strands, is uncertain.

The drama focuses on a few weeks defined by a feud between the Achaean leader Agamemnon and his greatest warrior, Achilles (the son of Thetis, a Nereid [sea nymph] and Peleus, the King of Phthia). In a tale of high drama, plots and counter-plots, and epic battles, Olympian gods and goddesses take their place alongside mere mortals. Achilles, for example, specifically seeks out the help of Zeus, the most powerful of all the gods. The bickering and feuding between deities all contributes to the fluctuating fortunes of those fighting in the human realm. Homer was perhaps the first to breathe discernible life into the array of divine figures that bestrode the Ancient Greek world, a contribution that alone changed the nature of storytelling in the classical world.

The *Odyssey*, the partner work to the *Iliad*, subsequently tells of the journey of Odysseus, King of Ithaca, as he makes for home after the fall of Troy – a trip that takes him ten years, as long as the war itself. His peril-strewn journey sees him face myriad challenges and setbacks, including the loss of his crew and encounters with, among others, the one-eyed Cyclops, the dangerous sirens luring seamen to their fates, and the Laestrygonians, a race of man-eating giants. All the while, Odysseus's wife and son, assuming that Odysseus is dead, fend off a succession of unsuitable contenders to marry the apparently widowed queen. A central theme of both works is the influence of fate on the destinies of both humans and gods. While both the earthly and divine maintain agency and freedom of choice in the day to day, the overarching narratives of life are deemed to be pre-set so that trying to evade one's fate becomes not only a vain enterprise, but a cowardly and foolish one too.

In some respects, the question of whether or not Homer was the single author who committed these epics to writing hardly matters. What is ultimately important is that the works themselves exist, that they altered the direction of world literature and that they continue to engage readers almost three thousand years after they were first written. Nonetheless, the question of disputed authorship always delivers delicious mysteries to ponder. It is widely accepted that both works date to a similar period, around the eighth or seventh centuries BC. However, some scholars contend that the two poems are the product of different authors, or perhaps even groups of writers working together. The predominant mode of cultural communication in the period was oral transmission, and many academics suspect that the *Iliad* and the *Odyssey* represent the literary gathering together of potentially multiple stories that had previously spread through the spoken word or song. The truth is that we know virtually nothing of Homer as a historical personality, and the few shards of pseudo-biographical information we do have, such as that he was blind, are highly questionable. The pair of poems deal with questions of memory and of the passing on of wisdom through the generations, so perhaps it makes most sense to think of Homer as a cipher for the bringing together – the memorialization – of long literary heritages into coherent, brilliant new works. The *Iliad* and *Odyssey* can be regarded not as the creations of a single great mind but as the extraordinary fruit of a cultural zeitgeist.

THE TROJAN HORSE

The *Odyssey* briefly mentions a military tactic that has come to captivate the imagination of generations of readers, but largely because of its more detailed retelling in Virgil's *Aeneid*. The Trojan horse was a giant wooden horse built by the Greeks and hauled into Troy by the Trojans as an apparent symbol of their military victory. Little did they know that a band of Greek soldiers was hidden inside. Once within the city, they sprang from the horse to open the city gates and let their comrades in – a move that led to the final sacking of Troy.

The impact of Homer was immediate and long-lasting. The depictions of the godly realm, for instance, quickly changed the way the Ancient Greeks thought about religion, the gods and goddesses becoming less abstract and more relatable. The descriptions of military battles were also absorbed into the Greek psyche, influencing approaches to tactics and even the psychology of war. The poems soon became vital tools of education, not just as literary models but as jumping-off points for wider philosophical and ethical debates. As Plato would put it, Homer 'has taught Greece'.

The Homeric epics introduced a new mode of dramatic storytelling that quickly spread beyond the boundaries of the Hellenic world. It is very much in evidence in the works of the great Roman poets like Virgil and Ovid, the former regularly being accused of purloining the *Iliad* and reconfiguring it into the *Aeneid* in the first century BC. But Homer's reach has been still longer, reaching to Shakespeare, for instance, who mined similar source material (albeit with a very different spin) for *Troilus and Cressida*. There are those who suggest that even the modern cinematic masterpiece of the *Star Wars* saga owes a large debt to the tradition of the Homeric epics.

The *Iliad* is an epic in every sense. In the dramatic story it relates. In the spellbinding language it uses. In the existential questions it poses to its audience. In making us see the world in a different light – as the critic Longinus put it in the first century AD, 'in recording as he does the wounding of the gods, their quarrels, vengeance, tears, imprisonment, and all their manifold passions Homer has done his best to make the men in the *Iliad* gods and gods men'. But perhaps most importantly, the *Iliad* reminds us that stories may be entertainments and may sometimes seem frivolous – all of which is fine – but at their best they bring an audience together in the most unexpected ways and help us come to a better understanding of who we are and what is our place in the world. No one prior to Homer had ever quite achieved that on such a scale or in such a masterly way.

TITLE: *AESOP'S FABLES*

AUTHOR: AESOP (ATTRIBUTED TO)
DATE: *C.* SEVENTH/SIXTH CENTURIES BC

. . . .

Generations of children – and adults – have grown up on a diet of ancient fables that impart wisdom in short, memorable and often highly entertaining illustrative tales. Now well over two thousand years old, these fables have proven they have staying power even if their origins are shrouded in mystery. Whatever the circumstances of their creation, their almost universal appeal over such a long period suggests that while much divides us as a species, there is also a seam of commonality – a shared well of ethics and ideas – that ultimately helps to unite us. So it is that stories like 'The Tortoise and the Hare', 'The Ant and the Grasshopper' and 'The Boy who Cried Wolf' have secured a global audience.

We can be sure that Aesop's fables originated in Greece around the sixth or seventh century BC, but beyond that there is little certainty. We do not even know if there was such a figure as Aesop or, if there was, whether he was responsible for the composition of the fables. It is possible he merely served as a figurehead, the purported author of what were in fact the fruits of many storytellers' labours. There are even doubts as to whether anyone could be said to have 'created' the stories, or whether it was instead a case of gathering together a collection of tales passed from generation to generation orally, which were constantly changing and evolving.

Whatever the truth, a figure called Aesop and described as a writer of fables was mentioned by Herodotus as early as the fifth century BC. He is there too in the works of Aristophanes at about the same time, while Plato reckoned that Socrates reworked some of the fables into verse while he was imprisoned for offending the Athenian authorities. Several hundred years later, an anonymous author composed an apparent biography of Aesop, which claimed he had been a slave from the Aegean island of Samos.

Born mute and cursed with ugliness, the story says, Aesop was very smart and full of wisdom, so that he grew to become celebrated across Greece, earning a small fortune in the process. However, when he visited Delphi and the locals declined to pay him for his displays of sageness, he insulted the city's people. They took revenge by accusing him of being a thief and, having planted the necessary evidence on him, sentenced him to death. The biography culminates with Aesop meeting his end in a fall from a cliff top, either at the hands of his accusers or in a bid to escape them. It all makes for a terrifically exciting story, but its veracity is highly uncertain. Today, most academics favour the notion that Aesop is something of a symbolic author, who became credited with any story that fitted into the general fable format.

ANCIENT HISTORY

Aesop had literary precursors in the Ancient Sumerian civilization. The Sumerians, often considered the first urban civilization and based in a region between the rivers Tigris and Euphrates, were composing their own fable-style stories as early as 1500 BC. These tales shared common features with Aesop's tales, such as the use of anthropomorphized animal characters to communicate a basic moral or piece of worldly advice, like the sage observation which echoes that in 'The Boy who Cried Wolf': 'Tell a lie and then tell the truth: it will be considered a lie.'

Notably, in their earliest iterations, the fables were regarded as serving an adult audience, reflecting social, political and religious considerations of their time. Although not philosophical works in the mould of a Plato or Aristotle, these sometimes-whimsical narratives – often featuring animals imbued with human characteristics – were regarded as vehicles for grand themes. A famed Athenian statesman, Demetrius of Phalerum, brought together the first known collection of Aesop's *Fables* in the fourth century BC with a view that aspiring orators should study them. Once they were translated into Latin around the first century AD, they became essential study materials for the educated classes of the Roman world too.

For centuries to come, the fables were delivered to a primarily adult audience, not least by preachers looking to impart parables rich in moral wisdom. It was the philosopher John Locke in the seventeenth century who seems to have been the first to spot their cross-generational potential. The *Fables* are, he said, 'apt to delight and entertain a child ... yet afford useful reflection to a grown man. And if his memory retain them all his life after, he will not repent to find them there, amongst his manly thoughts and serious business.' Louis XIV of France in due course incorporated a series of statues based on several of the fables into the design of his palace at Versailles, where he hoped they would contribute to the education of his young son.

It is their adaptability that has contributed to the longevity of the stories. By dealing in simplicity – of story and of message – they allow for the widest reception. They have served audiences across borders and of various religious faiths at vastly different historical moments. The Ancient Greek philosopher, the medieval Islamic scholar, the Reformation monk, the Enlightenment thinker, the Victorian moralist and the twenty-first-century educator have all been able to utilize the fables for their own purposes.

It is only in more recent centuries that the 'moral' of each story has tended to be included as part of the text. Yet many of those simple messages, even as they evolve and adapt to their audience, are as potent now as they were thousands of years ago. To this day, we sometimes need to be reminded of such simple truths as it pays to think before we act, that slow and steady wins the race, and that things are not always what they seem.

Apollonius of Tyana, a first-century-AD philosopher from Anatolia, sums up the simple magnificence of those stories (numbering over seven hundred) commonly attributed to Aesop:

> ... like those who dine well off the plainest dishes,
> he made use of humble incidents to teach great
> truths, and after serving up a story he adds to
> it the advice to do a thing or not to do it. Then,
> too, he was really more attached to truth than
> the poets are; for the latter do violence to their
> own stories in order to make them probable; but
> he by announcing a story which everyone knows
> not to be true, told the truth by the very fact
> that he did not claim to be relating real events.

TITLE: THE TORAH

AUTHOR: MOSES (ATTRIBUTED TO)
DATE: c. SIXTH/FIFTH CENTURY BC

. . . .

The Torah is a sacred book of the Jewish faith, consisting of the first five books of the Tanakh (the entire Hebrew Bible, which also includes the 'Writings' ('Ketuvim') and the 'Prophets' ('Nevi'im'). It is also sometimes referred to by the Greek name Pentateuch (Five Books). Tradition says that the Torah was written down by Moses after God communicated its contents to him on Mount Sinai. That would suggest a dating somewhere around the second half of the second millennium BC. Others hold that it is the product of multiple authors and the date of its production is uncertain, although there are references to a scribe called Ezra reading from the books in the fifth century BC, not long after the time of the Babylonian captivity.

Written in Hebrew, the Torah comprises the same five books that make up the start of the Christian Old Testament (itself equivalent to the Tanakh). These are 'Bereshit' ('Genesis'), 'Shemot' ('Exodus'), 'Vayikra' ('Leviticus'), 'Bamidbar' ('Numbers') and 'Devarim' ('Deuteronomy'). It begins with God's creation of the world and the Fall of Man, leading on to the emergence of the people of Israel, their exodus into Egypt and subsequent enslavement, Moses' encounter with God on Mount Sinai when he receives the Ten Commandments, the covenant between God and the

Jewish people, their forty years in the wilderness, and Moses' death just as the promised land of Canaan comes into view.

SCROLL UP, SCROLL UP

In 2014, a fifteenth-century copy of the Torah was put up for auction and achieved a record price of US$3.87 million when it was bought by an anonymous bidder. The book was printed in Bologna in January 1482 and, according to the auctioneers Christie's, represented 'the very first appearance in print of all five books of the Pentateuch as well as the first to which vocalization and cantillation marks have been added'. The back of the book, printed on vellum, carried the signatures of three censors active in the sixteenth and seventeenth centuries and confirmed that the volume had been housed in an Italian library at the time. The previous record for a Hebrew book had been US$2.41 million for an ornately embellished prayer book made in Florence in the fifteenth century.

As well as providing the origin story of the Jewish people, the Torah also provides guidance on God's laws (there are over six hundred commandments across the five books) covering ritualistic practice, civil laws and moral obligations. As such, the Torah is central to Jewish life in general, and not just in regard to religious observance. The Torah as used in worship takes the form of a hand-inscribed scroll (Sefer Torah), although it is more usually studied or privately read in book form. It is customarily read at the synagogue on Monday, Wednesday and the Sabbath (Saturday), as well as on assorted holy days throughout the year. The entire scroll is read in sequence during the course of the year, beginning at the festival of Sukkot in September or October.

Given its sacred status, the production and handling of the Torah is governed by numerous rules. While early versions were written on papyrus, most for use in worship are inscribed onto kosher animal skins (usually those of a cow). The text on a Sefer Torah must be written out in faultless Hebrew and devoid of any of the indicators of how each word should be pronounced so that the faithful must have pre-existing knowledge of the text if they are required to recite it. Each page of parchment (subsequently joined together into a scroll) has 42 lines and the entire Torah is made up of 304,805 letters. Should a scribe (or sofer) make a single mistake in producing the text, they are obliged to start the entire process again.

Once completed, the scroll is kept in an Ark (effectively a cupboard at the front of the synagogue shielded behind a curtain). When it is to be read from, it is laid out on a reading desk (*bimah*) and then lifted by the handles above the head of the reader so that all may view it. Each Torah is not merely a copy of the sacred text, but a sacred object in itself. For instance, if a scroll is accidentally dropped, the entire congregation may be obliged to fast for forty days. Moreover, the artefact plays a prominent role in other ceremonies, such as the Bar Mitzvah 'coming-of-age' ritual.

As the foundation document of the earliest of the three great Abrahamic religions, the Torah has not only served as a spiritual guide but as a formative influence on Jewish society and global history for well over two thousand years. Hillel the Elder, a Jewish religious leader who was born in Babylon around the first century BC and was living in Jerusalem in the time of King Herod, commented: 'That which is hateful to you, do not do to your neighbour. That is the whole Torah; the rest is the explanation.'

TITLE: *THE ART OF WAR*

AUTHOR: SUN TZU (ATTRIBUTED TO)
DATE: *C.* SIXTH–THIRD CENTURY BC
. . . .

The Art of War is the earliest known treatise on military tactics, attributed to Sun Tzu ('Master Sun'), who was traditionally thought to have lived in the sixth century during China's Spring and Autumn Period (named after the *Spring and Autumn Annals*, a classic work documenting the period 722–481 BC). However, there are significant questions as to the author's identity and many scholars consider the text was likely written at a later date. What is more certain is that *The Art of War* has been a vastly influential work in terms of martial strategy, both in Asia and, in more recent centuries, across the world. The first and perhaps greatest volume on military science, the many lessons it offers have been extrapolated for use in other disciplines too, from sport and business to personal development.

The work is divided into thirteen chapters, each focusing on a different skillset, for instance detailing approaches to terrain, espionage, planning an attack, starting a battle, moving troops and attacking with fire. According to Sima Qian's first century BC *Records of the Grand Historian*, a work widely understood to be *The Art of War* was in circulation by around 500 BC and attributed to Sun Wu, a military theorist who apparently fled his own state of Qi in favour of the kingdom of Wu. Wu's king, it was said, read Sun Wu's work and admired it greatly, crediting it with training even the 'dainty ladies' of the court in the ways of war. The parallels between Sun Wu and Sun Tzu are obvious. However, there is little else in the historical record to support Sima Qian's account, which has led some historians to speculate that the volume was actually written as late as the fourth century BC, perhaps by an author named Sun Bin, during the turbulent Warring States Period.

Many of the tactics described are simple and timeless. Yet for all that they might seem obvious, they are none the less powerful for that. Tried and tested over millennia, the genius of Sun Tzu (or whoever the author may be) is that he formally recognized their power so long ago. Underpinning the treatise are principles that may be paraphrased as: prepare properly and strike when you are strong and your enemy is weak. 'There are five essentials for victory,' the book states. 'He will win who knows when to fight and when not to fight. He will win who knows how to handle both superior and inferior forces. He will win whose army has the same spirit regardless of rank. He will win who, prepared himself, waits to take the enemy unprepared. He will win who has military capacity and is not interfered with by the sovereign.'

Numerous of *The Art of War*'s instructions and nuggets of advice have become accepted as fundamental tenets of the lexicon of war. Take, for example, the adage: 'If you know the enemy and know yourself, you need not fear the result of a hundred battles. If you know yourself, but not the enemy, for every victory gained you will also suffer a defeat. If you know neither the enemy nor yourself, you will succumb in every battle.' Or the admonition not to rest on one's laurels but always to be developing new approaches: 'You do not win in battle the same way twice.'

BOWLED OVER

When it comes to American Football and the National Football League, there has never been a more celebrated coach than Bill Belichick, winner of six Super Bowls as head coach of the New England Patriots. His coaching philosophy, he has publicly stated, is based on *The Art of War*, and the Patriots' locker-room is emblazoned with one of its quotations: 'Every battle is won before it is fought.' 'You can go all the way back to a few hundred years BC, Sun Tzu, *The Art of War*,' he has said. 'Attack weaknesses, utilize strengths and figure out what the strengths are on your team. There are some things you have to protect. Find the weaknesses of your opponent, and attack.'

Another vital component of the underlying philosophy is that, ideally, war should be avoided. Conflict, the book says, should always be the last resort, turned to only when all diplomatic avenues have been exhausted. Then, it is the job of military leaders to plan and fight thoughtfully and strategically so as to minimize the damage caused and the resources exhausted. It is easy to see why such ideas still resonate so strongly today. 'Troops that bring the enemy to heel without fighting at all – that is ideal,' Sun Tzu urged.

If indeed the Wu king was won over by *The Art of War*, he was only the first of many. In 1080, when the book was already some fifteen hundred years old, the Song emperor Shenzong formally adopted it into the Chinese literary canon, naming it as one of the 'Seven Military Classics'. To win promotion to certain imperial positions, it was required reading alongside the likes of the *Analects* of Confucius.

Nor was the fame of the book constrained to China. For example, in sixteenth-century Japan, Takeda Shingen, a leading feudal lord (*daimyo*) in the Kai Province (modern-day Yamanashi Prefecture), had an impeccable reputation as a military leader and garnered the nickname 'The Tiger of Kai'. Known for ruthless efficiency in battle and a strategic approach to his rule off the battlefield, he was profoundly influenced by *The Art of War*. His battle standard was emblazoned with the phrase 'Fu-Rin-Ka-Zan'. Translating as 'Wind, Forest, Fire, Mountain', it derived from Sun Tzu's concept: 'Swift as the wind, Silent as a forest, Fierce as fire, Immovable as a mountain'. Into the twentieth century, diverse figures such as China's Communist leader Mao Zedong, Vietnamese general Võ Nguyên Giáp and Norman Schwarzkopf, leader of the coalition forces during the 1991 Gulf War, were all students of the book. Mao is reported to have said: 'We must not belittle the saying in the book of Sun Wu Tzu, the great military expert of ancient China.' General Douglas MacArthur, the American Supreme Commander for the Allied Powers during the Second World War, also acknowledged that 'I always kept a copy of *The Art of War* on my desk', while Colin Powell –

variously Chairman of the Joint Chiefs of Staff, National Security Advisor and the US's first African-American Secretary of State – noted: 'I have read *The Art of War* by Sun Tzu. He continues to influence both soldiers and politicians.'

Today, you are as likely to find a quotation from the work at the start of a business book or wellbeing guide as in a military treatise. It has regularly infiltrated the world of sport too, where high-stakes competition frequently has the air of war without the killing. In 2002, Luiz Felipe Scolari led the Brazilian national soccer team to victory in the World Cup and it was reported that he posted extracts from the book under his players' doors during the night. In an article for the *Irish Times* in 2018, General David Petraeus, a noted US serviceman and later director of the CIA, put it succinctly: 'Sun Tzu's classic work is, in short, a fascinating mixture of the poetic and the pragmatic, and every bit as relevant now as when it was written.'

TITLE: *ANALECTS*

AUTHOR: CONFUCIUS
DATE: COLLECTED FIFTH–THIRD CENTURIES BC

. . . .

The *Analects* are the collected sayings and thoughts of the great Chinese philosopher, Confucius. The book post-dates Confucius himself (551–479 BC), and was likely initially compiled by his followers at some stage during China's Warring States Period (475–221 BC) before taking the form with which we are familiar today under the Han dynasty (202 BC–AD 220). Often characterized as the epitome of 'Eastern wisdom', Confucianism revolutionized Chinese – and wider Asian – civilization by promoting a code of conduct demanding correct behaviour in both the public and private spheres. His teachings continue to wield significant influence today.

He was born Kong Qiu at Qufu in the Lu state of China in 551 BC. The name 'Confucius' is in fact a Europeanization of one of his later official titles, Kong Fuzi – Master Kong. His life coincided with a period of upheaval as the relative calm of China's so-called Spring and Autumn Period gave way to the more troubled Warring States Period. His family enjoyed moderate wealth and prestige, and when he was still not yet twenty years old, he became a civil servant in the Lu court, where he emerged as a diplomat of rare skill. There he developed a model of secure, moral, centralized government that would underpin much of his wider philosophy. However, he was unable to entirely sidestep the constant wave of dynastic disputes brewing between the leading aristocratic families, and he eventually went into voluntary exile in 497 BC, during which time he travelled widely and worked as a teacher before returning to Qufu, where he died in 479 BC. This almost two decades away from home ensured that few of his ideas came to fruition in his own life, so it fell to later generations to take up his mantle.

In pursuit of fair and just government, Confucius emphasized the links between personal conduct and the wider social good. He confronted Chinese tradition by disputing that power and virtue are divinely bestowed on an elite. Instead, he regarded humanity as an agent of divine will, charged with creating moral order. Virtue, he said, is not given but cultivated. He argued that everybody, regardless of their social station, could behave with virtue and benevolence and thus have a role to play in developing the social structure. Moreover, he believed that judgement and wisdom are more important than unthinking obedience to rules, and that those with power ought to set a moral example. 'Exemplary persons,' he said, 'help out the needy; they do not make the rich richer.'

For a region long used to living with a strict social hierarchy, such theories were inflammatory. That is not to say, though, that he was entirely a radical. Many aspects of his outlook on social affairs were highly conservative. For example, he demanded observance of traditional rituals and ceremonies (such as ancestor worship) and the practice of filial piety, while also urging individuals at every social level to accept their status and fulfil their role to the best of their abilities. He envisaged a society based on reciprocal relationships: where a sovereign should be benevolent, his subject must be loyal; a parent loving, and a child respectful; a husband fair, his wife understanding. Take, for instance, his following aphorism: 'At home, a young man should be a good son, when outside he should treat others like his brothers, his behaviour should be trustworthy and proper, and he should love the multitude at large and keep himself close to people of benevolence and morality. If after all these activities, he has any energy to spare, he should read widely to stay cultivated.' By doing right, Confucius argued, we shall be treated rightly in return, and thus society becomes intrinsically fairer. In the words of his 'Golden Rule': 'Do not do to others what you would not have done to yourself.'

Key to the Confucian belief system is the idea of sincerity, of which he said it is 'the end and beginning of things; without sincerity there would be nothing'. 'Sincerity becomes apparent,' he taught. 'From being apparent, it becomes manifest. From being manifest, it becomes brilliant. Brilliant, it affects others. Affecting others, they are changed by it. Changed by it, they are transformed. It is only he who is possessed of the most complete sincerity that can exist under heaven, who can transform.'

The 'Doctrine of the Mean', a key text of Confucianism probably written by his grandson Zisi, put it like this: 'Sincerity is the way of Heaven. The attainment of sincerity is the way of men. He who possesses sincerity is he who, without an effort, hits what is right, and apprehends, without the exercise of thought; he is the sage who naturally and easily embodies the right way. He who attains to sincerity is he who chooses what is good, and firmly holds it fast.'

Confucius was also interested in questions of knowledge and wisdom. 'To know what you know and know what you do not know – this then is wisdom,' he concluded. He considered education bred confidence, which in turn bred hope, which itself brought peace. He also urged that we learn from mistakes and, crucially, rectify them since by not doing so is to commit another mistake. 'By three methods we may learn wisdom,' he claimed. 'First, by reflection, which is noblest; second, by imitation, which is easiest; and third by experience, which is the bitterest.'

ENDURING APPEAL

Confucius may represent the wisdom of the ancients but he continues to attract new followers. In 2009 the Holy Confucian Church was founded by Zhou Beichen, a student of the noted modern-day Confucian disciple Jiang Qing. The first church was based in Shenzhen, one of China's largest cities. A national entity, the Holy Confucian Church of China, appeared six years later with the ultimate aim of establishing Confucianism as a state religion.

In the centuries immediately after Confucius's death, great weight was given to the so-called *Five Classics* that Confucius was held to have written and edited (although their authorship is now much disputed). These were the *Classic of Poetry*, the *Book of Documents*, the *Book of Rites*, the *I Ching* (or *Book of Changes*) and the *Spring and Autumn Annals*. The

Analects were long thought of as rather secondary, serving as a mere commentary on these other works. But over time, it is the *Analects* that have been most widely absorbed. The oldest-known extant copies, both dating to *c.* 50 BC, were discovered at locations in Hubei Province and Pyongyang in North Korea, in 1973 and 1992 respectively.

Their influence extended to Europe in the seventeenth century when they were introduced by Jesuit missionaries working in China. Voltaire was among those to take notice, commenting: 'Confucius has no interest in falsehood; he did not pretend to be a prophet; he claimed no inspiration; he taught no new religion; he used no delusions; flattered not the emperor under whom he lived …' But it is in East Asia that Confucius's ideas have had most impact (even when out of favour for a large part of the twentieth century under China's communist regime) – not only in China, but in Japan, Korea, Singapore, Vietnam and elsewhere.

TITLE: *THE REPUBLIC*

AUTHOR: PLATO
DATE: *C.* 375 BC
. . . .

The Republic is the most famous treatise of Plato, one of the three behemoths of Ancient Greek philosophy alongside his teacher Socrates and his student, Aristotle. Written in the early part of the fourth century BC, it considers models of the ideal city-state and questions what constitutes a just polity and a just individual. Plato also introduced his concept of 'Ideal Forms' in the work, which ponders the nature of reality. While many of *The Republic*'s core ideas have been disregarded by mainstream philosophy in the millennia since, its methodology and dazzling intellectual virtuosity have informed the discipline more than perhaps any other work. In 2001, a poll by *Philosophers' Magazine* of over a thousand philosophers and academics found *The Republic* to be the greatest work of philosophy ever written.

Plato was born in Athens around 428 BC, into a high-ranking family with access to the very best education. It is suggested that he was born Aristocles and that Plato, meaning 'broad', was a nickname, perhaps in recognition of his stocky build and wide forehead, or alternatively as a nod to the breadth of his knowledge. He studied under Socrates in his hometown but left after his master's execution in

399 BC on charges of corrupting the city's youth with his teachings. Plato then spent several years travelling abroad but returned to Athens in 385 BC and set up his legendary Academy, where new generations of notable thinkers – Aristotle among them – received the benefit of his wisdom. *The Republic* was written in the decade or so after the founding of the Academy.

The Republic is structured as a Socratic dialogue between Plato's former teacher, Socrates, and several other philosophers. With none of Socrates' own writings having survived, Plato essentially preserved his master's ideas in the many dialogues he wrote. In fact, academic debate continues to rage as to where Plato's ideas begin and Socrates' end in these texts. The dialogue is a vehicle for the Socratic (or dialectic) Method perfected by Socrates – a form of inductive argument in which a subject, concept or argument is investigated through a series of questions and answers. By thorough cross-examination, the durability of the argument or concept under investigation is thoroughly tested. If it collapses under questioning, it must either be discarded or else revised and re-tested. The knowledge of the participants is thus increased until they arrive at an idea that is shown to be resilient even under intense scrutiny. For example, in one of Plato's dialogues, Socrates asks his companion Euthyphro to define piety. Euthyphro argues that whatever is pious is beloved of the gods, but Socrates counters that the gods are prone to quarrel in respect of objects of love or hatred. Therefore, a thing might exist that is loved by some gods but hated by others. According to Euthyphro's definition, an object can thus be pious and impious all at the same time – an absurd illogicality. And so the search for a new definition begins. Socrates likened himself to a midwife whose task was to birth ideas.

Despite his adoption of the dialectic method, Plato nonetheless had a very different conception to Socrates as to the ways in which one can arrive at knowledge. Key to Plato's philosophy was his Theory of Forms. He contended that a realm of idealized forms exists separate to the material world. Moreover, our souls (which he considered the seat of reason, while our material bodies are the seat of the senses) existed in this realm prior to their earthly manifestation, as a result of which we carry with us knowledge of them. So, for instance, we are born with an inherent concept of the ideal flower so that we can recognize a rose or an orchid or a poppy as variants of this form. And as for flowers, so too for dogs or colours or mountains or even concepts like justice and virtue. We judge, for instance, the virtue of another by comparing them to the ideal form of virtue we recognize in our souls.

The realm of the Ideal Forms, he suggested, is the 'real' world while our material world is made up of mere shadows of these forms. That is why, for example, Pythagoras could envisage a perfect triangle when no such thing exists in nature. Plato famously explored this notion of reality in 'the Allegory of the Cave' in *The Republic*. It describes a group of people who have spent their lives chained up in a cave, facing a blank wall, their necks manacled to fix their gaze. Behind them, a fire flickers as the shadows of puppets are cast onto the cave wall. This world of shadows becomes the prisoners' reality and we, Plato said, are like them, drawing our knowledge from the observations of shadows. Instead, he contended, the philosopher should rely on their reason to recognize the true, Ideal Forms of things, just like a prisoner liberated from their shackles and free to turn and see the light behind them. This view changed the direction of philosophical thought, moving the focus from observation of the world around us to rationalism: prioritizing internal reasoning since the 'truth' of the Ideal Forms exists within and not external to us.

SO LONG, SOLON!

The family of Plato's mother, Perictione, claimed descendancy from Solon, a noted lyric poet and social reformer. Living between 630 BC and 560 BC, he was one of the so-called 'Seven Sages' – a band of celebrated philosophers and statesmen in Ancient Greece. He was famed for his progressiveness, enacting laws designed to favour the poor and that cemented his city's democratic traditions. His verse, meanwhile, ranged from patriotic propaganda to graphic erotica. In his *Protagoras*, Plato acknowledged the association, describing Solon as 'our own'.

Written against the backdrop of democratic Athens' recent traumatic defeat by Sparta and its allies in the Peloponnesian War, *The Republic* sees Plato conclude that philosophers are best suited to holding power on account of having set out to gain understanding and knowledge of the world and morality. He called for the emergence of the philosopher-king: 'Until philosophers rule as kings or those who are now called kings and leading men genuinely and adequately philosophize, that is, until political power and philosophy entirely coincide ... cities will have no rest from evils ... there can be no happiness, either public or private, in any other city.'

He said that the philosopher-king must pass a series of tests in a process of education lasting until he is fifty years old. Moreover, common ownership should be adopted by the ideal society (removing the temptation to acquire private goods) and the ruler should seek to maintain social harmony and justice while eliminating any potential source of corruption.

Prior to *The Republic*, philosophy was essentially a divided discipline, looking either at the nature of things, ethics or politics. But Plato's masterwork provided a new overarching approach that brought all of these aspects together, along with others like psychology and epistemology (i.e. the theory of knowledge). Its power has never waned, even as its conclusions have been challenged. As British philosopher Alfred North Whitehead (1861–1947) memorably noted, Western philosophy is 'a set of footnotes to Plato'.

TITLE: *HISTORY OF ANIMALS*

AUTHOR: ARISTOTLE

DATE: *c.* 350 BC

. . . .

Aristotle was one of the three leading intellectual giants of Ancient Greek philosophy. His works are the product of an extraordinary intellect that ranged across myriad subjects – among them politics, ethics, metaphysics, logic, psychology, physics, zoology, rhetoric and aesthetics. As such, he has had a profound influence on virtually every major intellectual movement, certainly in the West, that has come since. To choose his *magnum opus* is, perhaps, a fool's errand, since any number of his known works (and there are a great many that have been lost) might qualify. Nonetheless, his *History of Animals* stands as a landmark enterprise, considered by many as the first major scientific study of life on earth and the foundation document for the discipline of empirical biology.

Aristotle was born in Stagira, Chalcidice (not far from Thessaloniki in modern-day Greece) in 384 BC. He perhaps developed an early interest in matters of the living world as a result of his father being a doctor in the court of the Macedonian royal family. Aristotle enjoyed an education open only to the privileged and, when he was seventeen, joined Plato's Academy in Athens – where he stayed for twenty years, first as a student and then a teacher. He seemed all set to replace the ageing Plato as head of the Academy, but at the last the position went to Plato's nephew instead.

Moreover, the political temperature at the time was rising in Athens, and Aristotle felt a growing anti-Macedonian sentiment. So, around 348 BC, he chose to leave the city and made for Ionia (a region of Anatolia's Aegean shore in what is now Turkey) and then to the island of Lesbos.

Here his passion for biology and the natural sciences could be fully explored. Where Plato had believed that knowledge and wisdom stems from the application of reason, Aristotle was certain that the study of nature would bring its own enlightenment. He began a systematic study of the indigenous flora and fauna, both on land and in the sea, for instance seeking out every example he could find of a particular species in order to draw general conclusions about the species as a whole. With his reliance on evidence-gathering and repeated observation to arrive at broader inferences, he prefigured the modern scientific method by the best part of two thousand years.

Aristotle wrote up his research in what became the *History of Animals* – the ancient world's greatest work of natural history, zoology and marine biology. Along with two later additional treatises – *On the Parts of Animals* and *On the Generation of Animals* – it is the most well known of his biological works, which account for about a quarter of his surviving writings. His broad methodology was to explore existing facts (in Greek, *hoti*) in a bid to explain their causes (*dioti*). In practice, this meant looking at animal anatomy and physiology, investigating the differences between body parts and other characteristics, and exploring modes of behaviour, while also considering what was the result of design and what had occurred through chance.

To this end, Aristotle practised several techniques that propelled natural history forward in exponential ways. For example, he created an extensive system of hierarchical classification that provided the basis of the taxonomy that we use in the modern world. Beginning with living and non-living categories, he then sub-divided the types of all living things into, for example, plants and animals, and the plants into herbs, trees and shrubs, and animals as dwellers of the land, air or water, and so on. Groups all have shared characteristics, so that to be categorized as a bird, for instance, a subject must be living and have wings, feathers and a beak. But Aristotle did not solely rely on physical characteristics for classification. Instead, he looked at four 'causes' to explain existence: what something is made of; the shape or form it takes; how it is created; and what its purpose (or *telos*) is.

GREAT TIMES

Following his time on Lesbos, Aristotle was invited to Macedonia by King Philip II. Aristotle was charged with the education of Philip's son Alexander, who would go on to become known as Alexander the Great, one of the most effective empire-builders in history. While at the Macedonian court, Aristotle also contributed to the education of two other kings-to-be: Cassander (who would rule Macedonia) and Ptolemy (a future Egyptian pharaoh). Aristotle would eventually fall out with Alexander, however, and it has even been suggested (although with scant supporting evidence) that he might have been involved in the ruler's death when he was aged only in his early thirties.

He also practised dissection, still in its infancy, as a means of better understanding the anatomy of the animals under his study, although his work detailing these examinations has been lost to us. Sometimes relying on others' accounts of creatures that they had observed (for instance, mariners and bee-keepers), Aristotle's conclusions were not always correct. But some of his analysis was extraordinary. His account, for example, of the colour-changing phenomenon of an octopus and his description of male river catfish guarding eggs in lieu of the mother was considered highly improbable until empirically proven in the modern age. The *History of Animals* vastly increased humanity's bank of knowledge about the physiology and nature of hundreds of different species.

More importantly, it laid out the basics of a system that biologists have worked within ever since – an evidence-based scientific approach that prizes observable phenomena over hypothetical theories. The living world became an environment not defined by superstition and folklore, but by rational investigation and analysis. After Aristotle, natural historians could not merely talk in terms of what they thought was going on, but needed instead to show it to be so.

Such was the impact of his work that it was not substantially superseded until the sixteenth century, when such lauded names from the world of zoology and biology as Conrad Gessner, Volcher Coiter, Guillaume Rondelet and Ulisse Aldrovandi were busy researching in their various corners of Europe, each of them familiar with and building upon Aristotle's efforts. William Harvey, best known for describing the circulatory system, was another who drew heavily on Aristotle's findings in his work in the field of embryology. Sir Richard Owen, the celebrated nineteenth-century English naturalist, was fulsome in his praise of Aristotle's achievements: 'Zoological Science sprang from his labours, we may almost say, like Minerva from the Head of Jove, in a state of noble and splendid maturity.'

TITLE: *THE ELEMENTS*

AUTHOR: EUCLID

DATE: *c.* 300 BC

. . . .

The Elements is arguably the most significant work of fundamental mathematics ever written, underpinning the teaching of the discipline until well into the twentieth century. Its basic principles went unchallenged until the emergence of Albert Einstein, and while the latter's *General Theory of Relativity* demanded a re-evaluation of Euclid's tenets, Euclid's principles remain vital components of mathematical understanding, even if their universality has finally been disproven.

We know very little of Euclid the man other than that he was active in Alexandria, Egypt, during the rule of Ptolemy I (*c.* 367–282 BC) and that he was seemingly known by (and slightly pre-dated) Archimedes. *The Elements* comprises thirteen books that investigate:

- Geometry (which comes from the Greek for 'measurement of the earth') – the mathematical branch that seeks to address questions of shape, size and space, as well as the relationship between points, lines, curves and surfaces

- Number Theory – the branch of mathematics dealing with the properties and relationships of numbers and integers

Euclid provided definitions and laid out assorted postulates and propositions, which he then sought to prove or disprove in a thoroughly modern, logical and scientific way.

As well as introducing his own concepts and theories, he drew on the work of others, including Plato and several of Plato's followers, perhaps most notably the mathematician and astrologer Eudoxus of Cnidus (whose works are now lost to us). Pythagoras and Hippocrates of Chios were also obvious influences.

Problems of length, area and volume had long impacted on daily human life. How could one trade wine, for instance, if neither the buyer nor seller could be sure how much drink they were dealing with? Or how could a tribe sensibly divide up a slab of land without knowing its area? From the ancient farmer and trader to the modern-day computer scientist or rocket designer, life makes a lot less sense in the absence of geometry.

People had been wrangling with these questions of geometry for thousands of years before Euclid, with the Ancient Egyptians and Babylonians notable for making strides forward in finding mathematical solutions. In the West, meanwhile, Thales of Miletus was using maths to establish the distance of ships from the shore by the seventh century BC. But it was not until Euclid that the mass of geometrical knowledge was assimilated into a unified, coherent system that set the benchmark of intellectual rigour for mathematicians of all branches for well over two thousand years. Where uncertainty had ruled, Euclid helped define mathematics as a discipline of clarity and certainty.

For example, when introducing his work on plane geometry, Euclid outlined five basic axioms (or postulates):

- A straight line may be drawn joining any two points

- Any straight-line segment can be extended indefinitely in a straight line

- With any straight-line segment, a circle can be drawn having the segment as its radius and one endpoint as its centre

- All right angles are equal to one another

- Where two lines intersect a third so that the sum of the inner angles on one side is less than two right angles, then the two lines inevitably must intersect each other on that side if extended far enough

The reach of his work has been vast, and began extending out into the known world very shortly after he finished it. However, in common with other classical works, it became lost to Western Europe for a number of centuries, only being rediscovered in the early twelfth century when an English monk, Adelard of Bath, made a Latin translation from an Arabic translation. (In the medieval Islamic world, such eminent thinkers as Omar Khayyam were well versed in the work even as it was absent in Europe.) First printed in 1482, *The Elements* has since been published in some one thousand editions and is thought to be

MAN OF MANY TALENTS

Omar Khayyam (who lived from 1048 to 1131 in Persia) was a giant of the medieval Islamic world, a monumental intellect whose work ranged from mathematics and philosophy to astronomy, history and literature. However, his fame in the West was only secured much later, when a collection of poems attributed to him, the *Rubáiyát of Omar Khayyám*, was published in English translation. Although his authorship is disputed (experts can reliably assign only a handful of the verses to him), what is more certain is his brilliance as a mathematician. Among his numerous achievements, he calculated the length of the year with remarkable accuracy, putting it at 365.24219858156 days.

the most widely distributed textbook in history. Such scientific and mathematical luminaries as Nicolaus Copernicus, Galileo Galilei, Johannes Kepler and Sir Isaac Newton all to some extent stood upon Euclid's shoulders, but his approach also influenced philosophers more generally, from Enlightenment figures such as Thomas Hobbes and the archetypal rationalist, Descartes, to later logicians like Bertrand Russell. Euclid's reliance on formulating testable theories shaped them all. Mathematician

Eric Temple Bell has even likened him to a cowboy trussing up a steer: 'This is the hog-tie, and it is what Euclid did to geometry.'

For some two thousand years, Euclid was considered the last word in geometry. Then Einstein proved that space can exist in non-Euclidian forms, as around the mouth of a black hole. But even Einstein acknowledged his predecessor's extraordinary contribution:

> Here for the first time the world witnessed the miracle of a logical system which proceeded from step to step with such precision that every single one of its propositions was absolutely indubitable – I refer to Euclid's *Geometry*. This admirable triumph of reasoning gave the human intellect the necessary confidence in itself for its subsequent achievements. If Euclid failed to kindle your youthful enthusiasm, then you were not born to be a scientific thinker.

TITLE: *BHAGAVAD GITA*

AUTHOR: VYASA (ATTRIBUTED TO)
DATE: *C.* **SECOND CENTURY BC**

. . . .

The *Bhagavad Gita* (which translates as '*Song of God*') is considered among the cornerstone texts of the Hindu faith, and a pivotal work in the history of Indian philosophy. Made up of eighteen chapters and some seven hundred verses, it forms part of the much larger epic poem, the *Mahabharata*. Its influence has extended far beyond India and it became much revered in the West too, not least because of the British imperialist presence in the country from the eighteenth century. India's leading champion of independence, Mahatma Gandhi, called the *Bhagavad Gita* his 'spiritual dictionary', while the country's first post-independence leader, Jawaharlal Nehru, commented: 'The *Bhagavad Gita* deals essentially with the spiritual foundation of human existence. It is a call of action to meet the obligations and duties of life; yet keeping in view the spiritual nature and grander purpose of the universe.'

The poem is structured around a dialogue between the central protagonist, a prince called Arjuna, and his charioteer, confidant and guide, Krishna. The story comes in the wider context of the *Mahabharata* ('*The Great Epic of*

the Bharata Dynasty'), which tells of the dynastic struggles between two family groups, the Kauravas and the Pandavas (from which line Arjuna comes), in a text that runs to some seven times as long as the *Iliad* and the *Odyssey* combined. At the start of the *Bhagavad Gita*, these two familial branches are about to go into battle at Kurukshetra (encompassing an area of modern-day Haryana and the Punjab). Arjuna, however, is hesitant, aware that he is about to go into conflict with family members, friends and even his own teachers. 'I would not like to kill these,' he says, 'even though they kill me.' Wracked with uncertainty, he seeks advice from Krishna.

What follows is a profound rumination on such themes as the destiny of the soul, *dharma* (cosmic truth) and universal harmony, and the duty to act. Krishna – who is revealed to be a mortal avatar of the god Vishnu – persuades Arjuna of the immortality of the soul and that his duty as a warrior is to fight, but to do so without seeking personal benefit, thus contributing to the right order of things. In making his arguments, Krishna brings together multiple strands of Hindu belief with aspects of numerous Indian philosophies, not least the Vedic and Yogic traditions. Arjuna's doubts about going into war, Krishna shows, are as a result of his incomplete understanding of the nature of things. *Dharma*, he teaches, comes with selfless action.

The *Bhagavad Gita* was written in Sanskrit, the ancient Indo-European language that came to be a liturgical language accessible only to an educated elite. According to tradition, its author was Vyasa (or, according to one legend,

HEAVYWEIGHT WORDS

On 26 February 2019, the world's largest copy of the *Bhagavad Gita* was unveiled at the ISKCON (International Society for Krishna Consciousness) Temple in New Delhi, India. Consisting of 670 pages and measuring 2.8 metres by 2.9 metres, it weighs in at an astonishing 800 kg. Published by the Bhaktivedanta Book Trust, it was printed in Milan, Italy, on paper that claims to be waterproof and untearable, and includes eighteen full-page illustrations. It was unveiled by the nation's prime minister, Narendra Modi, who has described the text as 'India's gift to the world'.

it was dictated by Vyasa to the elephant-god Ganesha, who broke off a tusk to use for its inscription). However, Vyasa is probably a symbolic author, with many scholars open to the idea that there were actually multiple authors. Similarly, assigning a precise date to the poem's creation is highly problematic, although it seems unlikely to pre-date the fifth century BC and most academics favour a date in the second or third century BC. With its elegant verse and dynamic setting, the *Bhagavad Gita* is sometimes regarded as a more user-friendly update of the older and denser

Upanishads, philosophical treatises that formed part of the *Vedas*, authored roughly between the mid-second and mid-first millennia BC.

Western scholars began translating the work in the eighteenth century, and its impact away from its indigenous home was instant. The great nineteenth-century Scottish philosopher and essayist, Thomas Carlyle, was among those who praised it, calling it 'a most inspiring book; it has brought comfort and consolation in my life'. It has been noted, too, that the Indian-born Rudyard Kipling's most famous poem, 'If', can be viewed as a distillation of the *Bhagavad Gita*'s central message, notably in the lines: 'If you can meet with Triumph and Disaster/ And treat those two impostors just the same / ... Yours is the Earth and everything that's in it.'

For Ralph Waldo Emerson, the American transcendentalist, it was 'the first of books; it was as if an empire spoke to us, nothing small or unworthy, but large, serene, consistent, the voice of an old intelligence which in another age and climate had pondered and thus disposed of the same questions which exercise us'. Nobel Laureate Hermann Hesse, meanwhile, described it as a 'truly beautiful revelation of life's wisdom which enables philosophy to blossom into religion'. And Aldous Huxley considered it in the context of 'perennial philosophy', a term coined by Gottfried Leibniz in relation to the idea that all philosophies share certain recurring concepts. The *Bhagavad Gita*, Huxley said, is 'one of the most clear and comprehensive summaries of perennial philosophy ever revealed; hence its enduring value is subject not only to India but to all of humanity'. Its words even came to Robert Oppenheimer, director of the Manhattan Project that birthed the atomic bomb, on the occasion of the first nuclear detonation test:

> We knew the world would not be the same. Few people laughed, few people cried, most people were silent. I remembered the line from the Hindu scripture, the *Bhagavad-Gita*. Vishnu is trying to persuade the Prince that he should do his duty and to impress him takes on his multi-armed form and says, "Now I am become Death, the destroyer of worlds." I suppose we all thought that, one way or another.

But perhaps the last word is best left to Gandhi, who found inspiration in the text throughout his fight for his nation's freedom:

> I find a solace in the *Bhagavad Gita* ... when doubts haunt me, when disappointments stare me in the face, and when I see not one ray of light on the horizon I turn to the *Bhagavad Gita*, and find a verse to comfort me; and I immediately begin to smile in the midst of overwhelming sorrow. My life has been full of external tragedies and if they have not left any visible and indelible effect on me, I owe it to the teaching of the *Bhagavad Gita*.

TITLE: *ON THE SUBJECT OF COOKING*

AUTHOR: MARCUS GAVIUS APICIUS (ATTRIBUTED TO)
DATE: FIRST CENTURY AD

. . . .

In the commercial world of books, it is a well-known fact that you're more likely to please your bank manager by publishing the recipes of a celebrity chef than the latest scribblings of a Nobel Prize Winner. Eating is one of the few truly universal activities and people cannot get enough of tomes instructing you how to cook the most delicious meals. But the hunger for cookery books is not a modern phenomenon. They have been with us for millennia in evolving forms. In ancient times, recipes were presumably communicated orally but the oldest-known cookery volume is the Roman-era *On the Subject of Cooking* (or *De re coquinaria* in Latin).

FOOD FOR THE MASSES

In 1845, an English woman called Eliza Acton published another landmark cookbook that was in certain respects the antithesis of its Roman counterpart. *Modern Cookery for Private Families* included recipes that were designed to cater for the middle classes rather than the wealthy elite. Acton introduced the British public to new, exotic ingredients including spaghetti and Brussels sprouts. A runaway success, it was also the inspiration for another book on food and other domestic affairs that quickly came to usurp it in popularity after publication in 1861: the legendary *Mrs Beeton's Book of Household Management*. For all Mrs Beeton's wisdom, however, she did recommend boiling pasta for an hour and three-quarters!

The precise origins of the book are shrouded in mystery. The oldest extant editions date to the ninth century AD, and it is thought that the collection of four hundred or so recipes was brought together in perhaps the fourth or fifth century AD. However, it is probable that this volume was based on a number of recipes gathered from several different chefs in the first century AD. Among the most famous gourmets of that period was one Marcus Gavius Apicius, to whom authorship of the book has traditionally been attributed. Indeed, the book itself is sometimes referred to as *Apicius*. Nonetheless, it is highly unlikely that he set out to write a cookbook in the modern sense.

Instead, he was probably one of the principal sources of the recipes, although many of these may in fact have been the work of chefs whom he employed. Apicius was a merchant whose wealth allowed him to enjoy the high life during the rule of Emperor Tiberius in the first half of the first century AD. He was noted for the lavish feasts he hosted, and may even have been paid by the Roman authorities to entertain visiting foreign officials. But where contemporaries regarded him as showing off the best of the Roman world, others have come to see the excesses he promoted as a sign of the Empire's imminent decline.

As well as knowing how to put on a good spread, Apicius was also famed for his deep knowledge of food. This extended to the production of ingredients as well as their preparation. These were not recipes for ordinary folk, but for the trained cooks employed by the wealthy elite of Roman society. Apicius's reputation was well established by the time Pliny the Elder wrote in his *Natural History* that he was 'the most gluttonous gorger of all spendthrifts'. Pliny detailed, for instance, how Apicius was reputed to have learned to prepare a sow so that its liver might be a delicacy. The process involved feeding the beast with large volumes of figs and then, just prior to slaughter, giving it honeyed wine. By the end of the second century AD, Tertullian called Apicius nothing less than 'the patron saint of cooks'.

On the Subject of Cooking is divided into ten sections, each dealing with a particular aspect of cuisine, including housekeeping, meat, vegetables, pulses, poultry and seafood. The vast majority of recipes include a sauce, typically made either with fermented fish or a type of grape syrup. What is not made very clear are the quantities of ingredients to be used and, frequently, the precise cooking techniques. Often, the advice comes in terms similar to 'cook until ready'. Moreover, the required ingredients were frequently highly exotic. Among the meats considered are dormouse, crane, peacock and ostrich. One recipe requires the cook to parboil a flamingo before finishing it off with leeks and a spicy sauce. (It is worth noting, too, that the volume includes a number of suggested remedies for stomach ache.)

The lengths to which Apicius would go in order to find the best and rarest ingredients was legendary. Athenaeus of Naucratis, a Greek writer of the late second/early third century, wrote in *Deipnosophistae* – his epic account of a series of banquets held in Rome and itself considered a valuable source of information on classical cuisine – that Apicius embarked on a long voyage to Libya in search of giant prawns. Unsatisfied by the specimens he was shown, he was said to have returned to Campania empty-handed and disgruntled, without even having gone ashore. Seneca, a close contemporary, related another story of how Apicius became embroiled in a bidding war for an unusually large mullet. His teachings around food and its consumption, Seneca suggested, had 'defiled the age'.

It is true that Apicius's name became shorthand for gluttony. Elagabalus (also known as Antoninus), Rome's emperor between 218 and 222, was noted for his own pleasure-seeking excesses. He was said to gorge himself on delicacies like camel heels, peacock tongues, nightingales, flamingos' brains and the heads of parrots in imitation of Apicius. But time eventually caught up with Apicius, whose wealth was depleted by his opulent lifestyle. Apparently fearful of having to live on limited means, he reputedly opted to take his own life instead.

How much of *On the Subject of Cooking* is the work of his own hand is moot, but what is certain is that the book that bears his name opens a window onto life among Rome's high society. Perhaps more importantly, it established that the book form was a vessel not only for high art and philosophy but for exploring more corporeal pleasures too.

TITLE: *GEOGRAPHIA*

AUTHOR: CLAUDIUS PTOLEMY
DATE: *C.* AD 150

. . . .

Geographia (literally, *The Geography*) was a landmark hybrid work by the celebrated Greek polymath, written around the middle of the second century BC. A mixture of philosophical treatise on the nature of geography and cartography, an atlas

NEW WORLD VIEW

In 1569, the Flanders-born Gerardus Mercator published a new world map projection entitled *Nova et Aucta Orbis Terrae Descriptio ad Usum Navigantium Emendate Accommodata* ('New and More Complete Representation of the Terrestrial Globe Properly Adapted for Use in Navigation'). Like Ptolemy's work, it proved a game-changer, its blueprint still evident in the maps we use today. Indeed, the nineteenth-century Scandinavian aristocrat and explorer, Adolf Erik Nordenskiöld, said that Mercator 'stands unsurpassed in the history of cartography since the time of Ptolemy'. In 1595, Mercator also coined the term 'Atlas' for a cartographical work when he published his *Atlas Sive Cosmographicae Meditationes de Fabrica Mundi et Fabricati Figura* ('Atlas or Cosmographical Meditations Upon the Creation of the Universe, and the Universe as Created').

and a gazetteer, it serves as an unparalleled summation of geographical knowledge up to that moment in time. Moreover, its influence on future geographers and cartographers was immense throughout both Christian Europe and the Islamic world well into the early modern age. *Geographia* has been pivotal in moulding how we see and conceptualize our world for well over one and a half thousand years.

Ptolemy was born around AD 100 and lived in or very near to Alexandria, the Egyptian city that was then under the hegemony of the Roman Empire. Living in Africa under Roman rule and writing in Greek, he was at the cusp of several intellectual traditions. Like other great intellects of the classical era, he worked across multiple fields, including astronomy, astrology, mathematics and even music. The author of numerous academic works, *Geographia* is one of three for which he is most famed, the others being the *Almagest* (which sought to solve questions about the motion of the stars and planets through mathematics) and *Tetrabiblos*, a treatise on astrology.

Geographia is made up of eight books divided into three broad sections. In the first book, Ptolemy considers the method behind his work – how he went about gathering and arranging the geographical and cartographical information in the other seven books. Maps had been in production for several centuries by the time he was writing, but he also considered approaches for creating better maps with more accurate projections.

Books II–VII serve as the 'gazetteer', a catalogue of those major places around the world then known to the Romans, complete with each location's latitude and longitude. The end of Book VII is taken up with consideration of a number of projections designed to allow for the most accurate possible depiction of a world map, while Book VIII comprises a

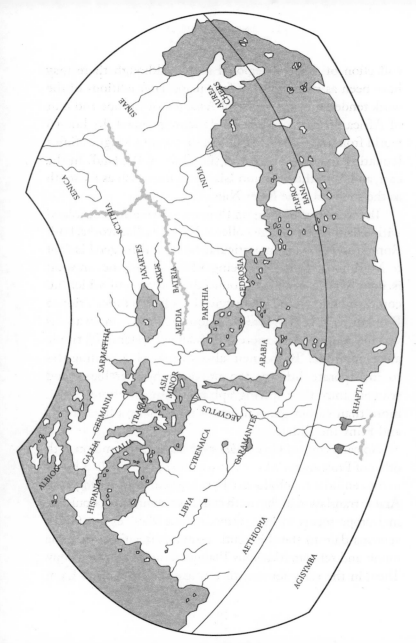

Ptolemy's landmark world map from his *Geographia c.* AD 150

collection of detailed regional maps. Although there may have been as many as sixty-four maps, later editions of the work tended to carry twelve of Asia, ten of Europe and four of Africa. In terms of extent, Ptolemy mapped the known world from the Canary Islands in the west to Magnus Sinus (equating today to an area in the Gulf of Thailand) in the east, and from the Shetland Islands in the north as far south as the sources of the River Nile.

The work was built upon Ptolemy's own ideas combined with existing knowledge collected from earlier works, both Roman and Persian. In particular, he acknowledged his debt to Marinus of Tyre (Tyre being a Roman province in what is now Syria), who had produced an atlas – of which no copies are known to have survived – a few decades prior to Ptolemy writing *Geographia*. Among Marinus's innovations was his adoption of a more fully realized system of latitude and longitude. Both men also displayed a willingness to incorporate information provided by merchants and seamen into their cartographical representations much more than earlier generations of map-makers like Strabo and Pliny the Elder.

No early copy of *Geographia* survives but, in common with other of Ptolemy's works, it was widely copied and distributed in the centuries that followed. It was certainly circulating in an Arabic translation in the ninth century, although its popularity in Europe seems to have waned. The earliest extant Greek versions date to the thirteenth century, after the Byzantine monk and scholar, Maximus Planudes, hunted down a copy. Then, in the early fourteenth century, the first major Latin translation was made by the Florentine humanist, Jacobus Angelus, under the title *Geographia Claudii Ptolemaei*. (An earlier translation from an Arabic manuscript undertaken for Roger II of Sicily in the twelfth century did not survive.) A print edition appeared in Bologna in 1477 and is thought to be the first printed book with engraved illustrations.

Angelus's work prompted a new interest in Ptolemy's cartography in the West, much of it having been long forgotten. Where medieval map-makers had, for example, given prominence to places according to their perceived importance, Ptolemy inspired a more scientific approach (albeit still laden with numerous errors) based on mathematics, more accurate measurement and greater consideration of projection. His gazetteer, meanwhile, restored knowledge of precise geographical locations that had long ago been lost to the Western world.

Renaissance Europe thus started to see the world drawn differently. To a modern eye, Ptolemy's world map is obviously flawed, both in terms of orientation and size. Yet it was infinitely more accurate than what had come before and, crucially, armed future cartographers with the tools to construct ever more accurate representations.

II

THE MIDDLE AGES

TITLE: THE QUR'AN

AUTHOR: ASSOCIATES OF THE PROPHET MUHAMMAD
DATE: SEVENTH CENTURY

. . . .

The Qur'an is the primary sacred text of Islam, the youngest of the three largest Abrahamic religions. Muslims consider the Qur'an to be the literal word of God, communicated directly to Muhammad by the archangel Gabriel between 610 and 632. Tradition has it that scribes among Muhammad's Companions (i.e. followers) then committed these divine revelations to paper. Aside from its religious status, it represents arguably the pinnacle of Arabic literary attainment and is undoubtedly among the most influential books ever written.

Muhammad was born in Mecca (an oasis city in what is now Saudi Arabia) and worked as a trader. Mecca at the time was subject to many polytheistic beliefs, but was also home to the Ka'bah, a cube-shaped shrine said to have been built by Abraham as a place of worship to God. Muhammad hailed from a clan that had responsibility for protecting the shrine. According to tradition, Gabriel first appeared to Muhammad in a cave called Hira on Mount Jabal al-Nou during the month of Ramadan in 610. Muhammad, who was aged forty at the time, was in the habit of coming to the cave alone to pray. Further visitations followed over the ensuing years, with Muhammad telling of how the revelations sometimes came like the ringing of a bell while at other times Gabriel appeared as a man and spoke to him.

It has been widely speculated that Muhammad was illiterate so that he recited Gabriel's messages to his Companions, some of whom memorized them while others committed the words to parchment, stones, the stalks of palm leaves and even the shoulder-blades of camels. At that time, the oral transmission and memorization of verse and stories was widespread. Muhammad was thus regarded as a vessel for the words that emanated from God himself, and so the faithful believe that the text of the Qur'an is not suitable for revision by human hand. The revelations ended in 632 with the death of Muhammad. Exactly when the entirety of these revelations was gathered together as the Qur'an is a subject of debate. Zayd bin Thabit, one of the Companions, is often credited with compiling the contents of the various oral and written sources into a single volume. As Islam spread to new regions with their own languages, a standardized edition of the Qur'an was ordered by Caliph Uthman ibn Affan by about 650, within two decades of Muhammad's passing.

The Qur'an consists of some 6,236 verses (*ayahs*) across 114 chapters (*surahs*), which may be categorized as either Meccan or Medinean depending on whether they pre- or post-date Muhammad's move to Medina in 622, when he set up a Muslim community free from religious persecution. While it is strictly forbidden for the Qur'an to feature figurative images, many editions boast ornate decoration in the Islamic style, which leans heavily on geometric designs, floral motifs and exuberant calligraphy. In terms of content, it is considered by believers to be the definitive word on all matters spiritual and secular, guiding aspects of life from one's relationship with God to earthly laws and practices, including the timetabling of prayer, eating and fasting, pilgrimage, the giving of alms, the outlawing of usury, laws relating to marriage and divorce, appropriate punishments and so on.

While the existence of many branches of Islam indicate that the words of the Qur'an inspire a multitude of interpretations, the words themselves are sacrosanct. The text also acknowledges a relationship with the founding scriptures of the other major Abrahamic religions, but considers that Moses and Jesus – while they were prophets who received the word of God – are secondary to Muhammad. Jesus, for example, is described as human, not the Son of God as Christians hold. Emphasizing its monotheistic precepts, the Qur'an believes in the divine's unity of being and transcendental nature that has a shared legacy with both Judaism and Christianity but which believers consider to have reached its zenith with Muhammad.

While Muhammad initially had just a small coterie of followers, mostly family and friends, Islam spread rapidly, especially after the migration to Medina (an event known as the Hijrah). By 630, Muhammad and his Companions had won control of Mecca while retaining their base in Medina. By the 660s, Muslim rule had extended far beyond the Arabian peninsula, encompassing large parts of

the Near and Middle East, North Africa and Central Asia.
At the heart of the burgeoning empire was the Qur'an and
its teachings.

AN OLD SURVIVOR

In 2015, a researcher at the University of
Birmingham in the UK began investigating
fragments of a Qur'an that had long been
gathering dust amid a collection of three
thousand documents from the Middle East
collected by a Chaldean priest, Alphonse
Mingana, in the 1920s. Carbon dating
showed the two leaves of parchment to date
from between 568 and 645, with a probability
of more than 95 per cent. This would make
the fragments the oldest-known examples of
Qur'an text in existence, the previous record
being held by the 'Tübingen Fragment',
dated between 649 and 675. It also raises the
real prospect that it was written by the hand
of someone who knew Muhammad himself.

As a work of literature, it is imbued with all the finest
traditions of Islamic poetry, its poetic nature regarded as
evidence of its divine provenance. Indeed, the reciting aloud
of the text remains an integral part of Islamic ritual. The

very word 'Qur'an' derives from the Arabic for 'to recite'. There is in fact a discipline, *tajwid*, devoted to teaching the rules governing correct recitation of the Qur'an, including the proper pronunciation of words, where to pause and resume, and how to ensure the musicality of the language. The link between divine revelation and poetical expression is made explicitly within the text, with those who opposed Muhammad said to have dismissed his teachings as merely 'the utterances of a poet'.

It is possible to argue that the Qur'an has never wielded more influence than it does today, with close to 2 billion Muslims in the world. The precise interpretation of its words is at times a ferociously contested question, sporadically with significant geopolitical ramifications. It is unquestionably a work that has melded the global landscape for the past millennium and a half, and looks all set to continue to do so.

TITLE: *BOOK OF KELLS*

AUTHOR: JEROME OF STRIDON AND
UNIDENTIFIED MONKS
DATE: *c.* 800

. . . .

Described by the eleventh-century *Annals of Ulster* as 'the most precious object of the Western world', the *Book of Kells* is not merely a relic of extreme beauty but also shines a light upon the spiritual life of Christian Europe in the medieval period. An illuminated manuscript of the four Gospels (translated into Latin) along with accompanying texts and tables, it was created by monk scribes and artists around the beginning of the ninth century.

What stands out in the *Book of Kells* is its extraordinary illustration across 680 pages, a near flawless example of the so-called Insular style that dominated British and Irish monasteries between the sixth and ninth centuries. It combines ornate calligraphy, traditional Christian iconography and distinctive interweaving patterns (for instance, Celtic knots) along with depictions of humans, flora and fauna (including cats and goats but, more exotically, peacocks and lions too), as well as mythological beasts, all shimmering with colour (many of them derived from exotic pigments). The first page of St John's Gospel, for example, consists of just four words ('*In principio erat verbum*' – 'In the beginning was the Word'), along with an illustration of a contemplative John, and then the image of a drunkard slugging back a goblet of wine while a red-tongued monster looms over him.

Authorship of the text is uncertain, although it is likely that at least four monks worked on the text and three on the design features, and perhaps many more. Each page has sixteen to eighteen lines of text, picked out in inks of black, yellow, purple, blue, green and red. Most of the text derives from the Vulgate, a fourth-century Latin translation of the scriptures completed by Jerome of Stridon, although some is taken from the earlier *Vetus Latina* translation.

The *Book of Kells* remains uncompleted, a considerable number of illustrations only present in outline. What is clear is that this was a major undertaking, a volume intended for ceremonial use, destined to live on the high altar and to be read from at mass. The cost in terms of material (aside from the inks, the pages are of expensive vellum, or calf's-skin parchment, and it is estimated that 185 calves were needed to provide sufficient material for all the folios) and man-hours would have been considerable. This was an object designed to inspire awe in all whose eyes fell upon it and to venerate the God whose truths the faithful believe it contains. From a time when we tend to think of Western Europe as being in darkness, the *Book of Kells* stands out as an immaculate jewel – a beacon of artistic expression fired by profound faith that tells us much of the mindset of the age. It also reflects the fact that, in the centuries following the collapse of the Roman

Empire, monks were now responsible for keeping alive the Latin language that had spread the word of Christianity in Europe.

Exactly where the book was created is uncertain. It is named the *Book of Kells* because it was kept for many centuries at the Abbey of Kells in County Meath, Ireland. The abbey was built in the early ninth century on the site of a former hill fort and dedicated to St Columba, a sixth-century Irish abbot and missionary who founded the famous abbey at Iona, an island off Scotland's west coast.

A THING OF BEAUTY

The years have not dimmed the book's ability to stun an audience. Since 1953, it has been bound in three volumes, two of which are on public display in rotation. One volume is customarily open at an illustrated page, while the other displays a double page of script. Despite having been shorn of some thirty pages, most of them in the medieval period, the artefact remains one of Ireland's biggest tourist attractions, receiving upwards of a million visitors a year.

There are numerous theories about how the book came to be at Kells. Some scholars have argued that it was produced in its entirety *in situ*, while others have suggested it was made partly or wholly at another monastery in England or Scotland (such as Lindisfarne – or Holy Island – in Northumberland) and later moved. The most commonly held thesis is that work was begun on Iona by Columban monks before the book was moved to Kells, perhaps to keep it safe from Viking raids – although Kells itself was the victim of a series of such raids in the period. With a little imagination, it is not difficult to picture those original Scottish monks bent over their painstaking work in their beehive-shaped stone huts on their weather-beaten island, carrying out their divinely inspired craft amid the elements.

The first documented reference to the book's presence in Kells comes only in 1007, when it is referenced in the *Annals of Ulster*. It had seemingly been stolen and its bejewelled golden cover removed before it was rediscovered after several months beneath a sod of grass. This incident may have resulted in the loss of a few pages at the beginning and end of the text. It then remained at Kells until 1654, when the forces of Oliver Cromwell rolled into town and the local governor took the doubtless wise decision to have the book moved to Dublin, where it might be stored safely. Seven years later, it was gifted to Dublin's Trinity College, which has been its permanent home ever since.

In 1188, the clergyman and historian Gerald of Wales wrote of the *Book of Kells*:

This book contains the harmony of the Four Evangelists according to Jerome, where for almost every page there are different designs, distinguished by varied colours. Here you may see the face of majesty, divinely drawn, here the mystic symbols of the Evangelists, each with wings, now six, now four, now two; here the eagle, there the calf, here the man and there the lion, and other forms almost infinite. Look at them superficially with the ordinary glance, and you would think it is an erasure, and not tracery. Fine craftsmanship is all about you, but you might not notice it. Look more keenly at it and you will penetrate to the very shrine of art. You will make out intricacies, so delicate and so subtle, so full of knots and links, with colours so fresh and vivid, that you might say that all this were the work of an angel, and not of a man.

TITLE: *THE PILLOW BOOK*

AUTHOR: SEI SHONAGON

DATE: *c.* 1002

. . . .

The Pillow Book is a collection of writings by Sei Shonagon, a member of the court of Empress Consort Teishi at the end of the tenth and beginning of the eleventh centuries. Its mixture of diary-style entries, personal musings and observations, and numerous lists provide us with a unique insight into Japanese courtly life at the time. It is the original, and finest, example of a work in the so-called *zuihitsu* style – a genre in which informal and often unconnected literary fragments are brought together in an ad hoc fashion, usually inspired by the author's personal experience and surroundings. But *The Pillow Book* has a perhaps even more important status for giving us a glimpse of the unguarded thoughts and feelings of a woman living in a period from which very few female voices reach us at all – let alone one expressed with such joyous freedom.

Of Sei Shonagon, we know very little – not even her real name. The moniker by which we know her would have been a courtly nickname. A *shonagon* was a relatively minor counsellor at the imperial palace, and her title suggests that she was probably married to such a figure. It is likely that she was married at least twice. She herself was born around 965 into a family of courtiers who never attained the highest level of importance and who often struggled with financial difficulties. However, they were seemingly renowned as a literary family, with Sei Shonagon's purported father and her grandfather being famous poets.

According to court records and the few bits of biographical information that can be gleaned from her writings, Shonagon became a lady-in-waiting to Empress Sadako around 994. She seemingly felt self-conscious and out of place, choosing to hide herself and absorbing the goings-on of the court from a safe distance. 'When I first went into waiting at Her Majesty's Court,' she wrote, 'so many different things embarrassed me that I could not even reckon them up and I was always on the verge of tears. As a result I tried to avoid appearing before the Empress except at night, and even then I stayed hidden behind a three-foot curtain of state.' But she nonetheless quickly won the favour of the empress, who apparently enjoyed her wit and wisdom. By Shonagon's own estimation, she was good at gossip and chatter, all delivered in a pleasing voice. And it was not long before she was transferring her thoughts and observations to paper – an expensive resource supplied to her by the empress herself, who had come into possession of a bundle of notebooks that she didn't know what to do with.

Not everyone was enamoured of her, however. Murasaki Shikibu was a rival at court, serving another Empress Consort, Shoshi (as well as being the author of *The Tale of Genji*, also featured in this book). She considered Shonagon as gifted but weighed down with self-satisfaction and a desire to set herself apart from others. She was, Shikibu also claimed, frivolous and given to allowing her emotions to get the better of her so that she was 'bound to fall in people's esteem'. When the emperor abdicated in 1011 and the empress lost some of her power, Shonagon certainly seems to have found herself well down the pecking order, with tradition suggesting she became a nun somewhere in the suburbs of the imperial city, seeing out her days in poverty.

Yet whatever the end of her life looked like, *The Pillow Book* has ensured her immortality. (A 'pillow' in this period was not the soft head-support that we think of today, but would have been a wooden construction, often equipped with a drawer in which a journal or other reading material could be stored.) In over three hundred or so entries of vastly different extent – some just a line, others running to several pages – Shonagon laid out a world, both external and internal, for her readers. We learn much, for instance, about the customs and mores of high society in the Heian age, the period that ran from 794 to 1185 and that saw the Japanese capital transfer from Tokyo to Kyoto. This was a golden age of indigenous Japanese culture, which was highly prized at court and reflected a waning of Chinese influence. The latter aspect particularly worked to Shonagon's advantage. When she was writing, it was still customary for men to write using Chinese characters (signalling their high level of education), while women were free to write in their native Japanese (using a system called *hiragana*, in which symbols represented syllable sounds). Thus unshackled, female writers in Japan enjoyed a far greater freedom of expression and one that tended to attract a wider audience because of its better accessibility.

While Shonagon's take on court life is fascinating, it is her personal reflections and her often highly entertaining lists that give the work a thoroughly modern feel. She always claimed that she had begun writing *The Pillow Book* for herself alone, and a sense of spontaneity and liberation shines through her prose. What she writes feels unencumbered by a need to please an audience, and the fact that she wrote to please herself in turn pleases us. At one point, for example, she ruminates about how a preacher ought to be good-looking, since he must keep his audience's eyes focused on him as he speaks if they are properly to understand his worthy sentiments. Another time, she notes that 'a good lover will behave as elegantly at dawn as at any other time'. Elsewhere, under the heading 'Men Really Have Strange Emotions', she decries those men who love 'ugly' women in a tone redolent of a modern-day internet chatroom.

In one memorable entry, she relates her fury when she made a pilgrimage to a Buddhist shrine, only to find a throng of 'commoners' had got there before her and were prostrating themselves. They looked like 'basket worms ... in their hideous clothes', she vents, adding that she 'really felt like pushing them all over sideways'. But she is not all vitriol. She tells, for example, the sad story of a dog almost beaten to death after attacking the empress's cat, only to be allowed to return to the court where it received an imperial pardon and was rehabilitated by a group of sympathetic courtly ladies.

Despite her intended audience being herself, Shonagon's writings soon found their way into wider circulation – even before the volume was complete. Writing near its end, she described how a court official had visited her at home one day before she had the chance to secrete the journal away. This man grabbed it, refusing to hand it back and taking it away with him, only returning it much later. 'That, I imagine, is when it first began to circulate,' she concludes. 'As a matter of fact, I wrote down, in a spirit of fun and without help from anyone else, whatever happened to suggest itself to me.' History can only be grateful that she did.

STILL MY BEATING HEART

There are well over a hundred and fifty of Shonagon's famous lists in *The Pillow Book*, many of them idiosyncratic and enormous fun. Take, for example, 'Things That Make One's Heart Beat Faster'. These range from sparrows feeding their young, passing a place where babies are playing and sleeping in a room where fine incense has been burnt, to noticing that 'one's elegant Chinese mirror has become a little cloudy' and seeing 'a gentleman stop his carriage before one's gate and instruct his attendants to announce his arrival'. Her romantic soul is evident too in the last entry on the list: 'It is night and one is expecting a visitor. Suddenly one is startled by the sound of raindrops, which the wind blows against the shutters.'

TITLE: *THE TALE OF GENJI*

AUTHOR: MURASAKI SHIKIBU
DATE: EARLY ELEVENTH CENTURY

. . . .

The Tale of Genji is a work of fiction depicting life among the courtiers of Heian-era Japan, a period of high culture and political intrigue, where appearances mattered much. Its author, Murasaki Shikibu – a pen-name, her real name being unknown for certain – was herself a courtier, serving as lady-in-waiting to the Empress Consort Shoshi. Historical references show the work to have been completed by 1021 at the latest. The book's original manuscript – written on lengths of paper joined together and folded like a concertina – no longer exists but the work is regularly cited as the world's first novel. According to Nobel Prize-winning novelist Yasunari Kawabata: '*The Tale of Genji* in particular is the highest pinnacle of Japanese literature. Even down to our day there has not been a piece of fiction to compare with it.'

The book tells, first, the story of Hikaru Genji ('the Shining Prince'), son of the Emperor Kiritsubo and one of his more lowly concubines, before moving on to the sagas of two of his descendants, Niou and Kaoru. The character of Genji is widely considered to have been based on one of the ministers at court at the time. It is a long book, coming in at some fifty-four chapters spread over well in excess of a thousand pages in English translation. The language, often lyrical and poetic, can be dense for the modern reader unused to Heian idioms. But it does not lack in compelling narrative drive. At its start, Genji falls victim to political manoeuvrings that see him stripped of his place in the line of succession. The narrative then follows the handsome and lusty protagonist ('so beautiful that pairing him with the very finest of the ladies at the court would fail to do him justice') as he embarks on life as an imperial officer, tracing his many romantic episodes and casting an eye over the customs, practices and foibles of the aristocratic milieu he inhabits. On one level, the book serves as something of a Jane Austen-esque read for fans of medieval Japan, but it also functions as a critique of Heian society and its purported obsession with outward appearances over inner morality.

Murasaki Shikibu (or 'Lady Murasaki', Murasaki meaning 'Lavender') shares a name with Genji's principal romantic interest and is thought to have been born in the 970s into a minor branch of one of Japan's most powerful families at the time, the Fujiwaras. Her father was probably a mid-ranking official who, rarely for the time, permitted the education of his daughter. She subsequently appears to have married an older man who already had other wives, and she only started writing after his death. Her rise to fame as a poet, however, was rapid and she soon found herself if not a central figure at court, at least a welcome interloper into high society. From her position at its fringes, and with her Buddhist-informed outlook, she bore witness to the schemes and plots, the affairs and flirtations, the break-ups and fallings-out that defined court life. And then she poured them into *The Tale of Genji*. Although, it should be noted, some scholars suggest that certain passages, differing in style and tone from the rest of the book, may have been the work of other writers. It has also been speculated that the book's rather abrupt finale is an indication that it was unfinished.

In creating her masterpiece, Murasaki adopted many of those elements we associate with the modern novel. A central protagonist is vividly drawn with psychological depth, as are the leading members of a large supporting cast (numbering in the hundreds). The plot is episodic rather than progressive, but characters evolve in response to the action, and internal consistency is maintained throughout. Her themes, meanwhile, are emotionally engaging and dramatically tense. She explores, for instance, the nature of romantic love (including its disappointments), the inescapable pull of passing time and, not least, the sorrow that accompanies human existence. The prose style and certain structural features may be of their time (for instance, many characters are not named but are instead referred to by their social station or their function), but *The Tale of Genji* remains in key respects highly engaging and relevant for a modern audience.

GENRE-QUEEN

Murasaki Shikibu is renowned as the author of two other major works. First, a short collection of verse, *The Poetic Memoirs*, published around 1014. Then, *The Diary of Lady Murasaki*, a collection of diary entries written in the vernacular Japanese of the day and including letters and verse written during her time at court. It is here that we garner most of the biographical information known about her but also where one may read her critique of *The Pillow Book*'s author, Sei Shonagon. The Heian period was a golden age for Japanese women writers but it is clear that solidarity only went so far.

Although no original manuscript in Murasaki's hand has survived, an ornate twelfth-century picture scroll illustrating scenes from the book is designated a 'National Treasure'. The earliest extant manuscript was written by Fujiwara no Teika in the first half of the thirteenth century, at which time there were thought to have been a number of slightly differing versions of the book in circulation. The first English translation of sections of the book was completed by Suematsu Kenchō in 1882, but an almost full translation (by Arthur Waley) only appeared between 1925 and 1933. The first volume received a review in *British Vogue* from Virginia Woolf. She expressed wonder that Murasaki was '[gazing] from her lattice window at flowers which unfold themselves "like the lips of people smiling at their own thoughts",' while the ancestors of 'Tolstoy or Cervantes or those other great story-tellers of the Western world ... [were] fighting or squatting in their huts'. She continued:

All comparisons between Murasaki and the great Western writers serve but to bring out her perfection and their force. But it is a beautiful world; the quiet lady with all her breeding, her insight and her fun, is a perfect artist; and for years we shall be haunting her groves, watching her moons rise and her snow fall, hearing her wild geese cry and her flutes and lutes and flageolets tinkling and chiming, while the prince tastes and tries all the queer savours of life and dances so exquisitely that

men weep, but never passes the bounds of
decorum, or relaxes his search for something
different, something finer, something withheld.

Jorge Luis Borges was another admirer, noting: '*The Tale of Genji*, as translated by Arthur Waley, is written with an almost miraculous naturalness, and what interests us is not the exoticism – the horrible word – but rather the human passions of the novel. Such interest is just: Murasaki's work is what one would quite precisely call a psychological novel.'

TITLE: *MAGNA CARTA*

**AUTHOR: ARCHBISHOP OF CANTERBURY
STEPHEN LANGTON**
DATE: 1215

. . . .

Magna Carta (which translates from Latin as *The Great Charter*) is an agreement hammered out in the early thirteenth century by England's King John and a group of his fractious barons with a view to avoiding civil war. It was the product of political pragmatism, geared towards preserving the wealth and power of a political elite. But its impact has gone much further than any of its signatories could have dreamed. It is widely regarded as nothing less than the founding document of the democratic ideals and civil liberties that have underpinned much of the Western world in the eight hundred or so years since its creation.

King John had come to the throne in 1199, succeeding his brother, Richard I ('the Lionheart'). Richard's reign had been largely peaceful at home and reasonably prosperous as well. He spent most of his time abroad on Crusade, so the English barons could oversee domestic affairs with little interference from above. John, though, was a different sort of ruler. Believing in his divine right to reign, he sought to impose his will and, at the same time, to do everything possible to enrich the royal coffers. He ruthlessly extracted taxes due on inheritances, in lieu of military service and even on the estates of widows who remarried. His barons did not take kindly to his heavy touch and discontent among them grew rapidly.

Matters came to a head when John undertook a series of expensive forays into France, culminating in the loss of Brittany and Normandy in 1214. The country was divided between those barons determined to take John to task, those who stood loyal to the monarch, and the majority who did not wish to show their colours. By 1215, the most powerful religious figure in the country – Stephen Langton, Archbishop of Canterbury – felt compelled to intervene. On 15 June that year, the two sides met at Runnymede, on the River Thames between London and Windsor, to put their seals on a document drafted by Langton.

The agreement gave various assurances about the rights of the Church, taxation, access to justice and protection from illegal imprisonment. Nonetheless, the bickering continued, not least because the barons accused John of quickly disregarding his pledges, leading to the First Barons' War in which plans were made to replace John with the future Louis VIII of France. But John would be dead before the end of the following year (a victim of dysentery), to be replaced by his nine-year-old son, Henry III. The Charter went through a series of revisions and reissues over the next few years, most notably by Henry in 1225 – the version that went onto the statute books – and in 1258, when the 'Provision of Oxford' set out terms for a baron-selected Privy Council to advise the monarch and formalized the calling of parliament three times a year.

So, how did this all come to matter so much in the wider world? For all *Magna Carta*'s mention of 'community of the whole land' and 'consent of the kingdom', its real intention was to consolidate rule by a monarch supported by a social elite. Rights were extended to those considered freemen, but there was little to cheer the 'unfree' – those serfs and villeins who eked out an existence in the service of their lords, a class that made up over half the population.

TAILOR-MADE

Although the exact number is not known, it is thought that at least thirteen copies of the original Charter were issued in 1215 to various authorities. Today, though, only four remain, and only one of those with its seal. All remain in the UK, one at Lincoln Cathedral, another at Salisbury Cathedral and two at the British Library in London. These latter two were collected in the seventeenth century by politician and antiquarian, Sir Robert Cotton. It is thought one was donated to him by a lawyer, Humphrey Wyems, who discovered it in a London tailor's shop!

Yet the barons had done something remarkable, almost by default. Despite having scant interest in the plight of the common people, they set a number of crucial precedents and principles. First, they established that a monarch could not simply rule in any way they saw fit. A king (or queen) was accountable for their actions and could be made to answer to the law. In other words, the rule of law prevailed.

In a similar vein, freemen of the realm were entitled to expect that the law should be executed with 'due process' and that no one should be deprived of their liberty without that due process. Only three of the Charter's original sixty-three clauses remain enacted, but they include the following ground-breaking Clause XXIX: 'No free man shall be seized or imprisoned, or stripped of his rights or possessions, or outlawed or exiled, or deprived of his standing in any other way, nor will we proceed with force against him, or send others to do so, except by the lawful judgement of his equals or by the law of the land. To no one will we sell, to no one deny or delay right or justice.' By the mid-thirteenth century, it was understood that these rights should extend to every person, regardless of their social status.

In the seventeenth century, the English jurist Edward Coke leaned heavily on *Magna Carta* in drafting the 'Petition of Right', which sought to limit the powers of the Stuart monarchs. There are also clear echoes of the barons' agreement of 1215 in the British Bill of Rights (1688) and the US Bill of Rights (1791). It informed constitutions across the New World and is there too in landmark documents such as the Universal Declaration of Human Rights (1949). Not bad for a document agreed on the hoof to quell a little local discontent in England all those centuries earlier.

In the words of Sir Winston Churchill in his *A History of the English–Speaking Peoples* (1958): 'And when in subsequent ages the State, swollen with its own authority, has attempted to ride roughshod over the rights and liberties of the subject, it is to this doctrine [*Magna Carta*] that appeal has again and again been made, and never as yet, without success.'

TITLE: *THE DIVINE COMEDY*

AUTHOR: DANTE ALIGHIERI
DATE: 1320

. . . .

Dante Alighieri completed his epic, visionary three-part poem, *The Divine Comedy*, in 1320 after working on it for some twelve years. A rich allegory drawing on existing religious, classical and secular literary sources, the extraordinary first-person narrative tells of the protagonist's journey through the three realms of the dead: Hell (*Inferno*), Purgatory (*Purgatorio*) and Heaven (*Paradiso*).

The piece serves as a landmark in several respects. As a work of literature, it has a place in the very highest ranks and for seven hundred years has been a cornerstone of the Western canon, such that T. S. Eliot was moved to note: 'Dante and Shakespeare divide the world between them. There is no third.' (See *Dante in Love: The World's Greatest Poem and How It Made History* by Harriet Rubin; Simon & Schuster, 2004.) Dante's decision to write the poem not in the Latin favoured by other writers of the age but in vernacular Florentine marked a step-change in literary tradition, opening up the work to a much larger audience and helping to establish the foundations of the modern Italian language. But the poem also had a profound impact on the popular understanding of religious teachings. Dante was rooted (though not uncritically) in the Roman Catholic traditions that then dominated European life, and *The Divine Comedy* did perhaps more than even the Bible itself to mould perceptions of the afterlife, especially concerning the nature of Hell ('Abandon hope all ye who enter here').

Born in 1265, Dante grew up in the Italian city-state of Florence, which was at the time a hotbed of political intrigue. He became an apothecary, although this seems to have been as a way of entering one of the professional guilds necessary to build a political career rather than through any great passion to practise pharmacy. In addition, it probably appealed to his literary instincts, since apothecaries often doubled as booksellers. Although never in the forefront of his city's political life, he sided with its papal-supporting Guelph faction in the long-running conflict with the Ghibellines aligned with the Holy Roman Empire. After the Ghibellines were defeated, the Guelphs split into rival factions, resulting in Dante's exile from his hometown for a good many years, during which time he seems to have first conceived the idea of *The Divine Comedy*.

At first, though, it was not 'divine'. He called his work only *Comedia*, the *Divina* being added much later by another great Italian writer of the period, Giovanni Boccaccio. In terms of the poem's structure, the three books – or *Cantiche*

– total some 14,233 lines and a hundred cantos (33 each in 'Purgatorio' and 'Paradiso', and 34 in 'Inferno').

The action takes place between just before dawn on Good Friday and the following Wednesday in 1300, with Dante the Narrator enjoying the company of three guides on his spiritual journey. For the visits to Hell and Purgatory, he is accompanied by the great Roman poet Virgil, while his chaperone in Paradise is Beatrice, an idealized woman based on a real person Dante had known in his youth in Florence. He had romantically longed for her but she died at a young age.

The epic adventure begins with the famous lines:

> Midway upon the journey of our life
> I found myself within a forest dark,
> For the straightforward pathway had been lost.

So starts his descent into Hell, which is made up of nine concentric circles, each filled with a different 'class' of sinners (exponents, respectively, of lust, gluttony, greed, wrath, heresy, violence, fraud and treachery). Each pays the price for their crimes against God, the horrors of which are described in hauntingly graphic ways. The first circle, meanwhile, is Limbo, where the spirits of the unbaptized dead and 'virtuous' non-Christians reside, less violent than the other circles but eternally sad and without hope of ascending to Heaven. Indeed, this is where Virgil resides.

Next, it is to Purgatory, a steep climb up a mountain that encompasses seven terraces, each corresponding to a different one of the seven deadly sins. Here, Dante ruminates on the nature of sin and its roots in love – love that is deficient, disordered, perverted or in excess of what is moral. The ascent of Purgatory also presents the author with the opportunity to critique what he regards as the failings of the Catholic Church and to ponder on wider contemporary political issues, which provided Dante with a rich vein of subject matter given his experience of political exile.

CHAUCER

Dante's adoption of the vernacular was a landmark for not only Italian literature but for the language itself. His choice was pivotal in moulding the development of a national *lingua franca*. Geoffrey Chaucer, author of *The Canterbury Tales* – another of the touchstone works of world literature – is often credited with having done something similar for the English language when he chose to write in Middle English rather than the expected French or Latin. His near contemporary, Thomas Hoccleve, would describe him as 'the firste fyndere of our fair langage'. Yet Dante made his bold step almost eighty years earlier.

At the peak of the mountain, Dante and Virgil arrive at the Garden of Eden, a manifestation of the pre-Fall innocence that the trip up Purgatory is designed to recapture. Dante is then joined by Beatrice, who goes with him to Heaven, guiding him through its nine celestial spheres, all the way to the Empyrean – the seat of God (where St Bernard guides him for the very last section). Along the way, Dante meets several sanctified figures, including Thomas Aquinas, Saint Peter and Saint John.

As well as the obvious influence of the scriptures on this theological journey, Dante took inspiration from elsewhere too. The cosmological aspects of the work owe much to the ideas of Ptolemy, for example, while Aristotle served as Dante's philosophical bedrock. The influence of Homer and, of course, Virgil is clear as well. But Dante took his disparate influences and mixed them together to create something entirely unique and without precedent. For centuries – even now – our collective vision of Heaven and Hell tends to be rooted in what he presented in *The Divine Comedy*.

Its influence upon others that followed has been immeasurable. Dante's fingerprints are in evidence across vast swathes of the cultural production of both the Reformation and the Renaissance but they extend further too. One may wonder, for instance, whether John Milton could have written *Paradise Lost* without Dante having come before him. William Blake reintroduced the work to a new audience in the nineteenth century hungry for Romanticism, while modernists like James Joyce and T. S. Eliot also counted Dante among their formative influences.

Joyce even said: 'I love my Dante as much as the Bible. He is my spiritual food, the rest is ballast.'

Aside from the artistic merit of his work, Dante helped change the way literature was consumed. By writing in the vernacular, he won a much wider audience than if he'd written in the Latin of the elite. By daring to take this course, he paved the way for others too, not least Boccaccio and Petrarch. But in broader terms, *The Divine Comedy* can be seen as a leap forward towards the modern age. It is a product of bravery that melded religion, mythology and politics – the heavenly and the earthly – in the most striking verse, laying the path to a new sort of literature and way of seeing. The Argentinian writer Jorge Luis Borges makes the case succinctly, describing *The Divine Comedy* as 'the best book literature has ever achieved'.

TITLE: *JIKJI*

AUTHOR: BAEGUN

DATE: 1372

. . . .

Jikji is a collection of Buddhist teachings drawn together in the late fourteenth century by Master Baegun (1298–1374), a monk and chief priest of the Anguk and Shingwang temples in Haeju, a city located in what is now North Korea. *Jikji* is an abbreviated title of the full title of the work that may be translated as 'Anthology of the Zen Teachings of the Great Buddhist Priests'. Consisting of teachings, hymns, eulogies and poems sourced from a number of high-ranking figures in the Buddhist world, it is an edition of the book published in 1377 (five years after Baegun finished writing it) that ensures its place within this volume. As recognized by UNESCO in 2001, the 1377 edition is the world's oldest existing book printed with movable metal type. A full seventy-eight years before the appearance of Johannes Gutenberg's famous printed Bible, *Jikji* represents the moment when the literary form commenced its evolution from being a medium of the elite to a medium of the masses.

At the time Baegun was compiling *Jikji*, the Goryeo dynasty controlled the Korean peninsula and under them Buddhism prospered, winning recognition as the national religion. Baegun intended that his text should be used in the education of students getting to grips with the particular demands of Zen Buddhism. When he finished working on it in 1372, it was woodblock printed – that is to say, it was printed using a method in which a wooden block is carved in relief and coated with ink to create the desired print on a piece of paper or other suitable material. This was a method that had been in widespread use in China and throughout East Asia for some time.

Whereas woodblock printing is a 'fixed' system in which each part of a particular text is required to be carved into a block, movable type printing is much more flexible. It uses movable components, each representing a different letter or symbol, which may be arranged in racks to compose the text to be printed and which can then be rearranged to produce different text. The racks are then inked and pressed onto the material to be printed upon. According to Shen Kuo, a scientist and statesman who lived from 1031 to 1095 under the Song dynasty in China, movable type had been invented by a man of 'unofficial position' called Bi Sheng around 1040 using character types crafted from a mixture of baked clay and glue. While it is difficult to be sure of such claims, China was certainly using movable type forged from bronze in the twelfth century. However, it was almost exclusively used for official documents, such as money or government papers. It was instead the Goryeo dynasty that made the early strides in using the technology for cultural production. Unlike later European counterparts, these early Korean printers did not have machinery to press the movable type onto material but instead carried out the process by hand – an extremely time-consuming job. There were undoubtedly books printed in this manner prior to *Jikji* but none has survived.

THE DIAMOND SUTRA

In 1900, a monk called Wang Yuanlu was out walking by the Mogao Caves (also known as the Caves of a Thousand Buddhas) in Gansu, north-west China. On his route, he found a sealed cave and inside he discovered tens of thousands of manuscripts and other artefacts. Among them was a Buddhist text, translated from Sanskrit into Chinese, that has become known as the *Diamond Sutra*. Running at about six thousand words, it is contained on a 15-metre-long scroll and its name derives from its full title: 'The Diamond That Cuts Through Illusion'. Produced using the woodblock technique on 11 May 868, it is most notably the earliest known example of a printed book.

Jikji was published in two volumes, although only the second volume has come down to us. It was printed on paper using type almost 25 cm across and 17 cm down. Occasionally, lines run askew and some letters are printed in reverse or show other flaws. But that is not to decry the enormity of what it represents. The final page even includes publication details, so that we know it was published in the July of 'the 3rd Year of King U' (1377) at

Heungdeok temple in Cheongju, in modern-day South Korea. It appeared three years after the death of its author.

As the five-centuries-old Joseon dynasty was reaching its end in Korea in 1887, a Frenchman and keen book collector named Victor Émile Marie Joseph Collin de Plancy was working as a *chargé d'affaires* at the French Embassy in Seoul. *Jikji* came into his possession (through means unknown) and was brought to the attention of the wider Western world in 1901 when a French scholar of East Asia, ethnographer Maurice Courant, included it in his bibliography of Korean works. In 1911 it was sold by the famous Parisian auction house, Hôtel Drouot, to another collector, jeweller Henri Véver, who bequeathed it to the Bibliothèque Nationale de France on his death in 1950. Twenty-two years later, Dr Park Byeong-seon, an employee of the Library specializing in East Asia, formally identified *Jikji* as the oldest extant volume in the world printed using movable metal type.

The book's residency in Paris has been a subject of vexation to many Koreans, who believe their national treasure should be restored to its homeland. The authorities in France, meanwhile, claim that it represents a jewel of world culture belonging to no single country, and that the Bibliothèque Nationale is best equipped to ensure that it is maintained for future generations. In 2001, a century after its inclusion on Courant's list, *Jikji* was inscribed onto UNESCO's Memory of the World Register.

While ownership of the work is likely to remain a subject of heated debate, its place in the roll-call of human achievement is secure. Reusable type signposted the way towards mass distribution and consumption of knowledge, and *Jikji* is its most ancient example.

TITLE: *REVELATIONS OF DIVINE LOVE*

AUTHOR: JULIAN OF NORWICH
DATE: LATE FOURTEENTH/EARLY FIFTEENTH
CENTURIES

. . . .

Revelations of Divine Love catalogues a series of religious visions which the author believes to have imparted a greater understanding of the true nature of Jesus Christ, his sacrifices and the reasons behind them. Although such revelatory material is remarkable in itself, it was hardly unique in its time. But what sets this volume apart is the identity of its author. Julian was a woman and her *Revelations* are considered the oldest-known surviving literary work by a woman in the English language.

Very little is known of Julian herself. She was born in 1342 in Norwich, then a thriving commercial and religious hub in the east of England, but we are not even sure of her real name. 'Julian' is widely thought to be derived from the patron saint of the Church adjacent to which she lived in a cell as an anchoress – that is to say, someone who sets themselves apart from the secular world in order to live a life of ascetic religious devotion. She is sometimes referred to as

Juliana or Mother Julian, too.

Julian lived in a time of great religious and social turmoil. The dominant Catholic Church was in the midst of an internecine war, and her early years would have been marked by the horrors of the Black Death that overtook Europe in the 1340s and 1350s. In England, the resultant social upheaval would also lead to the Peasants' Revolt in the 1380s.

The *Revelations* are based on sixteen visions, or 'shewings', that Julian experienced over two nights in 1373. She was about thirty years old at the time and was confined to bed with an illness that she feared would end her life. Her sight was failing and she was struggling to breathe but as she endeavoured to focus on the crucifix that hung above her bed, she reported a sudden feeling of painlessness and calm. As the visions came upon her, she saw among other things Christ, blood trickling from his crown of thorns at the time of the Passion (those events at the end of Jesus's life and prior to the resurrection), as well as Mary, a figure of 'wisdom and truth' in Julian's words.

The 'shewings' confirmed in Julian's heart the loving nature of God, who she said represents all that is good for humanity. She wrestles in *Revelations* with complex philosophical questions, such as the nature of God's identity and why a benevolent deity allows the existence of sin and evil in the first place. She examines in detail Christ's suffering and pronounces her desire to suffer alongside him. But, ultimately, she comes to the conclusion that divine love is the driving force of everything. Strikingly, she also refers to Christ in terms of 'Mother', a gender role-reversal that was extraordinary for the time, linking Christ to the idea of 'the divine feminine'.

Her understanding of God's love and compassion is perhaps most famously explored in the following extract:

> And in this he showed me a little thing, the
> quantity of a hazelnut, lying in the palm of
> my hand, it seemed, and it was as round as any
> ball. I looked thereupon with the eye of my
> understanding, and I thought, 'What may this
> be?' And it was answered generally thus: 'It is all
> that is made.' I wondered how it could last, for I
> thought it might suddenly fall to nothing for little
> cause. And I was answered in my understanding:
> 'It lasts and ever shall, for God loves it; and so
> everything has its beginning by the love of God.'

> In this little thing I saw three properties; the
> first is that God made it; the second is that God
> loves it; and the third is that God keeps it.

Julian recovered from her illness within a few days, at which point she wrote down her account of the revelations in a short form. But she continued to revise the work over the forthcoming decades, producing a 'long version' of some eighty-six chapters – a work produced not in the Latin of church clerics but in the Middle English that ordinary people spoke. 'This is a Revelation of Love,' it begins, 'that Jesus Christ, our endless bliss, made in Sixteen Shewings, or Revelations particular.' She referred to herself as 'a simple creature unlettered', perhaps wary of offending the church authorities with what were, in truth, her radical words. Clearly, she was literate but it is highly possible that she was self-educated, since girls were routinely deprived of the educational opportunities afforded to boys (and then only boys of a certain class).

Julian probably died some time in the 1410s, and the *Revelations* did not enjoy a wide readership in her lifetime. Nonetheless, although her own manuscript was lost many centuries ago, in an age before printing, it was sufficiently in circulation that hand-written copies were made. Three comprehensive copies are known to have survived. Two reside in the British Library and a third, produced by a group of exiled nuns in Antwerp in the late sixteenth century, is housed in Paris at the Bibliothèque Nationale de France.

In 1670 an English Benedictine monk called Serenus de Cressy translated the 'Long Version' of the work from the Paris Manuscript, publishing it under the title *XVI Revelations of Divine Love, Shewed to a Devout Servant of Our Lord, called Mother Juliana, an Anchorete of Norwich: Who lived in the Dayes of King Edward the Third.* A spate of further translations appeared in the nineteenth and twentieth centuries as interest grew in Julian.

HERE COME THE GIRLS!

Julian was not entirely a female voice alone. Among those she helped to inspire was the Christian mystic, Margery Kempe, who visited Julian in her cell in 1413 and stayed for several days. They discussed Kempe's own religious visions and wider aspects of faith. In the 1430s, Kempe recorded an account of her life and spirituality, dictating it to scribes who wrote it down. The resulting *Book of Margery Kempe* has subsequently been regarded by some as the earliest known autobiography in the English language.

Julian died little heralded. Even where she was buried has not come down to us. But her legacy is significant. Her work continues to challenge and resonate. She provides us with an insight into the medieval mind but also considers the nature of faith and love in ways that matter as much in the twenty-first century as they did in the fourteenth. Crucially, she is a distinct female voice echoing back from an age when such voices were all but deprived of a platform. While Julian was devout in her faith, the very existence of her words posed a challenge of sorts to the dominant patriarchal ideology and structure of the established Church. She is a voice for the unvoiced, resounding down through the centuries.

T. S. Eliot is among those who considered her words worth repeating, using one of her observations in his poem 'Little Gidding'. (See *The Poems of T. S. Eliot Volume I: Collected and Uncollected Poems*; Faber & Faber, 2015.) Words that are, perhaps, a fitting memorial to Julian herself: 'All shall be well and all manner of thing shall be well.'

TITLE: THE GUTENBERG BIBLE

AUTHOR/PRINTER: VARIOUS / JOHANNES GUTENBERG
DATE: *c.* 1455

. . . .

The Bible is the most sacred text of the Christian faith, comprising the Old and New Testaments, themselves made up of a total of sixty-six books. The Old Testament equates to the Hebrew Bible, which was written over the course of many centuries up until the second century BC, while the books in the New Testament were composed roughly in the latter half of the first century AD. Since Constantine the Great adopted Christianity as the religion of the Roman Empire in the fourth century AD, Christianity has been numerically the world's biggest religion. As such, it is difficult to overestimate the influence of the Bible, not only on the spiritual life of billions, but in terms of its social, political and cultural impact too. Of all the many editions of the Bible, the Gutenberg Bible is among the most important since it also represents the introduction of movable metal type printing to Europe. As we have seen, Asia was already several decades ahead in such technology, but Gutenberg's contribution played its own significant part in shaping the future of the world.

Gutenberg was born in Mainz around 1400 and worked as an engraver, inventor and, of course, printer. While the genesis of his printing press is not clear, it seems that, after a number of commercial misadventures, he spent much of the 1440s perfecting it. Because of the lack of East–West cultural exchange, he did not build upon the existing Asian expertise but rather invented his own original system from scratch.

He perfected an alloy of lead, tin and antimony that allowed for the production of cheap, durable type, as well as a hand mould for casting it. He also worked on the creation of oil-based inks that, unlike the water-based ones in wide currency, would not simply roll off the type. In effect, he realized you needed something akin to a varnish to stain the pages, rather than an absorbable ink as had traditionally been used. He also took inspiration from agricultural presses to develop the printing press, taking out much of the time-consuming effort of having to hand-print. If he was not the first to join the game of movable type printing, he is arguably the single greatest visionary to have played it. The result of his efforts was the beginning of mass communication.

Gutenberg's press was up and operating by 1450, but it was his Bible of 1455 that stands as his masterpiece. Although no two copies were identical, they customarily comprised some 1,288 pages bound in two volumes, each page made up of 42 lines. Some were printed on paper, others on vellum (with some 170 calf skins estimated to have been required for a single edition). Some had their titles and marginalia printed in different-coloured inks, while later copies often had such details added by hand – presumably to cut the time and cost of production. Each copy sold for somewhere in the region of thirty florins – a small fortune (around three years' salary for a clerk) that meant most went to monasteries and universities, or, occasionally, to a super-wealthy individual. For such a landmark work, Gutenberg's

KING JAMES BIBLE

Another landmark edition of the Bible is the King James Version, which first came into print in 1611. In an age of intense religious disharmony, the edition was commissioned by James I of England (and VI of Scotland) in 1604. Its aim was to bring a uniformity to the scriptures, countering religious tensions by communicating the biblical message in language accessible to the population at large. The text was divided into chunks, each of which was translated by a panel of experts. The result is a work of intense poetry that is regarded as among the finest of any English-language work. It added a number of phrases to the English lexicon too, among them 'bottomless pit', 'eye for an eye', 'scapegoat', 'a law unto themselves', 'give up the ghost', 'Physician, heal thyself', 'the powers that be', 'the skin of my teeth' and 'vengeance is mine'.

Bible had a tiny print run, probably not exceeding two hundred copies in the first few years of production.

Nor did it do much for his bank balance, either. Setting up his business had taken years and was capital-intensive, meaning that he had to rely on a number of business partners. One of the most important was Johann Fust, who sued Gutenberg for non-payment of a loan related to the Bibles. Gutenberg lost and had to hand over much of his printing hardware as well as unsold copies of the book itself. The project put its creator on the brink of financial meltdown and it is unlikely that he ever turned any real profit from the undertaking.

Yet the quality of his work was recognized from the outset. Around the time that Gutenberg was being sued by his erstwhile investor, a Catholic priest called Enea Silvio Bartolomeo – who a few years later would be elected Pope, taking the name Pius II – saw some promotional pages in Frankfurt and reported on them to the Spanish Cardinal Carvajal in Rome. They were, Bartolomeo said, 'exceedingly clean and correct in their script, and without error, such as Your Excellency could read effortlessly without glasses'. Today, fewer than fifty copies of the Gutenberg Bible are known to survive, most in the possession of institutions. If they were expensive in their day, they are now virtually priceless. The last complete edition sold at auction was back in 1978, when it fetched US$3.3 million. A single volume went for US$5.4 million nine years later, and single sheets have sold for as much as US$150,000. Whether that would have delighted or infuriated the impoverished Gutenberg is uncertain.

Gutenberg's contribution to civilization is at least widely acknowledged now. By paving the way for the mass production of books in Europe, and by extension the New World, he was instrumental in producing a better-informed and better-educated populace. Without him, the Reformation, the Renaissance and the Age of Enlightenment would all have looked very different. It may even be said that the Gutenberg Bible was the gateway to the modern age. At the end of the last century, *Time Life* magazine went so far as to say that Gutenberg's technical innovations represented the pinnacle of human achievement in the last millennium. His Bible was a Good Book indeed.

NAME: MADRID CODEX

AUTHOR: UNKNOWN
DATE: *C.* FIFTEENTH CENTURY

. . . .

The Madrid Codex is one of just four surviving codices – or ancient books – dating from pre-Columbine times written in the hieroglyph script of the ancient Maya civilization. It is also the most extensive. One of the earliest writing systems known to humanity, the Maya script was virtually wiped out by the Conquistadors who overran large parts of central and south America between the sixteenth and eighteenth centuries. The Maya equivalent of the Rosetta Stone (pivotal in deciphering Ancient Egyptian hieroglyphs), the Madrid Codex has allowed for the unlocking of the lost language in recent decades. Bringing back to life one of the most significant advances in human history, the book also serves as a trenchant antidote to one of humankind's worst acts of cultural vandalism.

The Codex was found in Spain in the 1860s in two distinct parts, and it was only after some time that it was understood that they formed a unified work. It seems likely that the book found its way to Spain as a souvenir of one of the original Conquistadors. There has been much debate as to its date of production. Some have claimed it was not written until after the Spanish arrived but the consensus is now that it dates to the period before their arrival, possibly originating in Yucatán. Many Maya scholars ascribe a date of the fifteenth century, although others have suggested it might date as far back as the thirteenth. The early suspicion that it was post-Columbine was in part because a papal bull was affixed to the manuscript, although this may have been a much later effort by a Maya priest to have the document blessed.

The Codex is made from Amate, a paper derived from tree bark in a process practised in the Maya's sphere of influence for millennia. Some fifty-six sheets were folded up in concertina form and covered with a fine plaster-like substance onto which the hieroglyphs were painted. The subject matter is varied and includes details of religious rituals, horoscopes and astronomical tables. There are even illustrations of human sacrifice. There appear to have been multiple authors, probably from the priestly class.

The Maya had emerged as a major civilization by at least 2000 BC and, at its peak, tens of millions of Maya inhabited a large swathe of the Americas, covering modern-day Belize and Guatemala and parts of Mexico, Honduras and El Salvador.

Lesser known than their contemporaneous neighbours, the Aztecs, the Maya created an extraordinary cultural legacy based around their own highly idiosyncratic belief system. They were brilliant mathematicians, for example, and were among the first civilizations to explicitly adapt the notion of 'zero' into their counting system, no later than the mid-fourth century AD – more than eight hundred years before Europe caught up with the idea. They were brilliant architects too, building awe-inspiring cities deep in the jungle.

But their greatest intellectual achievement was the development of a complex written language using glyphs, some representing whole words and other sounds that can be combined to form words (and in some cases, glyphs that had both roles). Theirs was among perhaps the first four or five writing systems that the world had ever known, putting them alongside the likes of the Egyptians, Sumerians and Chinese. In the Americas, such a jump of imaginative thinking was entirely without precedent.

But the arrival of the Conquistadors proved devastating. Figures like Diego de Landa, the Spanish-born Roman Catholic Bishop of Yucatán, literally sought to erase their cultural heritage. Driven by an insatiable missionary zeal to convert the Maya away from their traditional beliefs, Landa and his like roamed the country looking for souls to 'save' and ungodly objects to destroy. To him, the Maya were pagans and, most devastatingly, practitioners of human sacrifice. He felt it his God-given duty to make them see the error of their ways. On 12 July 1562, for example, in the town of Mani on the Yucatán peninsula, de Landa ordered a conflagration, its flames

THE CODICES

Apart from the Madrid Codex, the three other authenticated Maya codices are:

- The Dresden Codex, identified as of Maya origin in the 1820s and dating from the thirteenth or fourteenth century

- The Paris Codex, discovered in 1859 and dating to no later than 1450

- The Grolier Codex, discovered in the 1960s and dating to the eleventh or twelfth centuries. This later document was only authenticated in 2018, in recognition of which it was renamed by the National Institute of Anthropology and History of Mexico as the Códice Maya de México

fuelled by over five thousand religious and cultural artefacts, including a unique library of books written in the Maya language. In de Landa's mind, this was an *auto-de-fe*, an 'act of faith'. 'We found a large number of books in these characters,' he would later write, 'and, as they contained nothing in which were not to be seen as superstition and lies of the devil, we burned them all, which they regretted to an amazing degree, and which caused them much affliction.' The efficiency of the destruction that he and others like him oversaw was daunting, but somehow a handful of Maya texts found their way to safety.

From the late sixteenth century, the Maya language was virtually lost to the world. It lived on in a meaningful way only in archaeological finds, especially in inscriptions on buildings and monuments. Gradually academics in the eighteenth and nineteenth centuries made some headway in reading these inscriptions but because they could decipher little other than the dates, the Maya earned a reputation for being obsessed by matters of the calendar. It was only in the 1950s that real progress in relearning the language began, in large part thanks to intensive study of the Madrid Codex and the other extant codices. It began to be understood that the Maya glyphs were not only emblematic but represented phonetic sounds. It was a gruelling process but the 1980s and 1990s were something of a golden age of Maya decoding, so that today scholars can read something approaching 90 per cent of extant Maya writing.

The Madrid Codex, kept at the Museo de las Américas in Madrid, has been crucial in that process. A fascinating text in its own right, shedding light on the customs, beliefs and practices of an ancient civilization, it is also integral to one of the greatest cultural renaissances ever seen. There remains a community of several million self-identifying Maya across the globe, and large numbers are now relearning their lost language. Five hundred years after it was apparently extinguished, the Maya language – one of ancient civilization's greatest achievements – is coming back to life.

III

THE EARLY
MODERN AGE

TITLE: *THE FOUR CLASSIC NOVELS*

AUTHOR: VARIOUS

DATE: FOURTEENTH–EIGHTEENTH CENTURIES

. . . .

The *Four Classic Novels* are a mini-canon of Chinese stories written during the reigns of the Ming and Qing dynasties between the fourteenth and eighteenth centuries. In terms of subject, they are disparate works and their precise authorship and historical origins are frequently subjects of debate. But as a unified body, they represent an extraordinary cultural achievement whose impact is wide-ranging. They have played a vital role in the creation of the Chinese cultural identity, although what they tell us about that identity has been and remains under almost constant reappraisal. They compel their readers to engage with profound issues of Chinese history – among them, the influence of Buddhism and Confucian dialectics, the cyclical nature of power and what constitutes good rule.

Technically, the novels are things of wonder, combining the influence of traditional, orally transmitted folk tales, ancient written histories and their own novelistic innovations (not least the melding of classical Chinese with vernacular forms) to create epics replete with memorable characters and highly involved storylines. The result is an invitation to examine personal ethics but also to undertake a moral critique of wider society. What does it mean, the novels ultimately ask, to be human and what sort of country should

China aspire to be? Quite the questions to ask of the world's most populous country and a major global power.

JOIN THE CLUB

Modern literary criticism sometimes expands the *Four Classic Novels* into a group of six. The additions are:

- *The Plum in the Golden Vase* by an unknown author using the pseudonym Lanling Xiaoxiao Sheng, 'The Scoffing Scholar of Lanling' (published c. 1610)

- *Unofficial History of the Scholars* by Wu Jingzi (published 1750)

Each of the novels is remarkably long, ranging from roughly eight hundred to two and a half thousand pages, ensuring that a brief synopsis can only provide an incomplete glimpse. Nonetheless, each work was written to stand alone and needs to be seen as such, as well as part of the quartet:

Romance of the Three Kingdoms. Written in the fourteenth century and widely attributed (though not without some dissent) to Luo Guanzhong, it tells the tale of the turbulent latter stages of the Han dynasty and the Three Kingdoms era (in which the states of Cao Wei, Shu Han and Eastern Wu vied for power), covering the period from around AD 169 until regional reunification in 280. The novel draws on history, myth and legend as it follows the fortunes of a cast of hundreds, including feudal lords and their vassals. The tale's opening line gives a sense of one of its overriding themes: the cyclical nature of power and the influence upon this of human ambition, loyalty and morality. 'The empire, long divided,' it begins, 'must unite; long united, must divide. Thus it has ever been.'

Water Margin. This was also written in the fourteenth century and is often attributed to Shi Nai'an, although its authorship is a subject of intense debate among experts. The events it depicts are set some two hundred years earlier in the period of the Song dynasty. It narrates the exploits of a group of 108 bandits who come together at Liangshan Marsh and who eventually secure an amnesty from the authorities in order to go off on campaign, battling rebel uprisings and fending off foreign attackers. The novel's most famous figure, Song Jiang, is a version of a true-life historical figure of that name, whose life was already the subject of much folklore. By the time the novel arrived, Jiang was well established as an outlaw-hero, righting wrongs and fighting for justice outside the law in a manner that has parallels to the English-language tales of Robin Hood. Bonds of brotherhood and male camaraderie are a central theme, often at the expense of women, who are largely depicted in an unsympathetic light amid some highly bawdy exchanges. The book's celebration of rebellion and outlawry led to its banning at certain points in its history.

Journey to the West. Widely thought to have been written by Wu Cheng'en in the sixteenth century, and arguably the best known of the *Four Classic Novels* outside of China, this was inspired by the seventh-century adventures of Xuanzang, a Buddhist monk who spent many years pilgrimaging to the 'Western Regions' (that is to say, the Indian subcontinent and Central Asia) in search of religious texts. Xuanzang recorded his travels, which saw him endure enormous hardships and face extraordinary challenges. The novel's lead character, Tang Sanzang, is assisted by a group of comrades, perhaps most famously the Monkey King. The novel's frequently comedic narrative addresses multiple themes. In terms of spirituality, it mingles aspects of mythology, Buddhism and Taoism, as well as traits of Confucianism and more localized religious belief systems. It also serves as a satire on bureaucracy and government.

Dream of the Red Chamber. Written by Cao Xueqin in the eighteenth century, this adopts a more realist tone than the rest of the quartet. It tells the story of an aristocratic dynasty divided into two houses, the narrative focusing on some forty main characters and a cast of several hundred supporting figures. Like *Romance of the Three Kingdoms*, it is interested in the nature of power (how it is both won and lost). It is also the most obviously 'psychological' of the four books, including subplots of romance, fraternity and tragedy. In parts loosely biographical, it is influenced by the author's own experience of growing up in a family in decline, and reflects the slow waning of the ruling Qing dynasty. It was a ground-breaking work in depicting characters of moral ambiguity and by using vernacular rather than classical Chinese. Indeed, Cao's employment of the Beijing dialect proved a significant influence on the development of Modern Mandarin.

The novel in the East had an evolutionary history distinct from that of the form in the West, but in both instances the form became an essential mode to examine the history and mores of the societies that produced them, and the moral and cultural dilemmas that their citizens faced.

The Plum in the Golden Vase gained notoriety for its sexually charged narrative but also represents a milestone in sophisticated storytelling that sees it lauded as a Chinese equivalent to *Don Quixote* in terms of literary importance. *Unofficial History of the Scholars*, meanwhile, is a searing satire of the academic world. As such, the *Four Classic Novels* are a potent window onto a vital civilization.

TITLE: *THE PRINCE*

AUTHOR: NICCOLÒ MACHIAVELLI
DATE: 1532

. . . .

Niccolò Machiavelli was a political operative who wrote his most famous, or infamous, work, *The Prince*, in a bid to curry favour with the powerful Medici family in his native Florence. It is arguably the founding document of *realpolitik* – in other words, politics based on practical objectives rather than ideals. It is in many ways the last word in pragmatism. Machiavelli was centuries ahead of his time, given that the term *realpolitik* was only coined by Ludwig von Rochau, a German statesman and writer, in the nineteenth century. Although Machiavelli never used the formulation, his central argument is often summarized as 'the ends justify the means' – an adage that has informed a host of subsequent political heavyweights (and many from other fields of endeavour as well) for better and worse.

MACHIAVELLIAN MACHIAVELLI?

Four years after *The Prince*, Machiavelli wrote *Discourses on the Ten Books of Titus Livy*. But now his tone had changed somewhat. 'The governments of the people are better than those of the princes,' he wrote. 'Only in those instances where there is insufficient social equality to establish a republic should a princedom be chosen.' What must the Medici have thought? Was *The Prince* perhaps not the product of its author's heartfelt convictions as much as a book designed to secure his own advancement? In other words, did Machiavelli practise a little disingenuousness to suit his own purposes? *The Prince* is itself an act of *realpolitik* …

Machiavelli was born in Florence in 1469, in the age of the all-powerful city-states in Italy. And few dynasties were more powerful than the Medici. They accumulated vast wealth and influence, coming to boast two popes so that their power base extended to the Vatican and incorporated the Church's vast reach. Such levels of success demanded the ruthless execution of power. However, the family also had its foibles – not least a taste for debauched living and a tendency towards corruption that made them a target for rival families. In 1513, the Medici had recently returned to power after almost eighteen years in exile and Machiavelli, who had previously worked as an ambassador for them, was keen to get back into their good books. He wanted to share the benefit of his experience with his Florentine overlords, to encourage a mode of rule that was rooted in real conditions rather than rarefied, abstract notions of what a ruler ought to be. In his own words: 'Many have imagined republics and principalities which have never been seen or known to exist in reality; for how we live is so far removed from how we ought to live ...'

To this end, he decided to write a treatise on governance, which would become *The Prince*. He based it on the observations he had made of the formidable Cesare Borgia – the Duke of Valentinois and illegitimate son of Pope Alexander VI – while working as a diplomat for the Medici over a decade earlier. Borgia had once been a cardinal but resigned from the Church to became a military general for France's King Louis XII, going on to conquer several of the Italian city-states and create a mini-empire of his own. Machiavelli had closely watched Borgia for several months and was struck by his changeability. One moment, he could be playful and charming, the next, moody, secretive and angry. He also managed to combine a talent for planning with an instinct for opportunism. Crucially, he could be utterly ruthless too. For all that Borgia was intimidating, Machiavelli admired him.

Taking Borgia as his model, Machiavelli contends that 'the Prince' (or indeed, any ruler) is morally free to do whatever is required to achieve his goals, however unpalatable those actions might be. He argued that a prince might resort to any action – even deception and murder – if by doing so he maintains the stability and security of his realm. If peace demands lying, then that is an acceptable price to pay. Such statements were an apparent repudiation of the Church's moral teachings and prompted uproar in Renaissance Italy, where Catholicism ruled supreme, leading the book to be banned until after Machiavelli's death.

Of course, he was not suggesting an automatic default to deception or brutality. He positively encouraged demonstrations of compassion and generosity to endorse public morality and as a means of consolidating support, thus reducing the likelihood of unrest. But he was clear that the prince's desire to be loved by his subjects ought to be secondary to his desire to be feared: 'it would be best to be both loved and feared. But since the two rarely come together, anyone compelled to choose will find greater security in being feared than in being loved … Love endures by a bond which men, being scoundrels, may break whenever it serves their advantage to do so; but fear is supported by the dread of pain, which is ever present.'

While the Medici warmly embraced the book, others were appalled. Francis Bacon wrote in his *Meditationes Sacræ* (1597) that the work ought to be read so that good people might defend themselves against evil:

We are much beholden to Machiavelli and
others, that write what men do, and not what
they ought to do. For it is not possible to join
serpentine wisdom with the columbine innocency,
except men know exactly all the conditions of
the serpent; his baseness and going upon his
belly, his volubility and lubricity, his envy and
sting, and the rest; that is, all forms and natures
of evil. For without this, virtue lieth open and
unfenced. Nay, an honest man can do no good
upon those that are wicked, to reclaim them,
without the help of the knowledge of evil.

The Prince continues to resonate as a philosophical work that
forensically examines certain long-held ethical assumptions
within a starkly realist context. After all, Machiavelli was
telling what most of us understand – that many of those
who attain and wield power are not benevolent but are
prepared to do much (if not absolutely anything) for their
own ends and for the benefit of their realm. It signposted
the way towards the philosophical pragmatism of Charles
Sanders Peirce and William James by several centuries in
its argument that good leadership is reflected not in the
good intentions of the leader but in the practical outcomes
of their action. It may also be seen as distinctly utilitarian in
its willingness to sacrifice the unhappiness of a few in the
interests of the many (as represented by the state). Better, it
might be argued, the extrajudicial deaths of ten conspirators
than the loss of thousands of lives in a civil war.

TITLE: *THE INGENIOUS GENTLEMAN DON QUIXOTE OF LA MANCHA*

AUTHOR: MIGUEL DE CERVANTES
DATE: 1605/1615

. . . .

'Somewhere in La Mancha, in a place whose name I do not care to remember, a gentleman lived not long ago, one of those who has a lance and ancient shield on a shelf and keeps a skinny nag and a greyhound for racing.' So begins *Don Quixote*, published in two volumes a decade apart, considered a shining beacon of world literature and often cited as the first modern novel in the Western tradition. It is a complex work in terms of both content and style. Ostensibly a comedic parody of chivalric romances, its intertextuality lends it an air of post-modernism too, despite it being created centuries prior to the invention of that term. Its author, Cervantes, had a mastery of language that puts him at the very forefront of his profession, his prose being inventive and playful. But aside from its significance as an early example of the novel, *Don Quixote* continues to resonate as a rumination on the human condition and how we strive to reconcile our dreams with reality. Over four hundred years after its publication, it is a novel with a genuine claim to timelessness.

Cervantes' own life story – much of it shrouded in some mystery and lacking in detail – has elements of the picaresque. Born in 1547 into a family that frequently found itself in debt, it seems he had to leave Madrid (where the family had settled) in 1569 after injuring another man in a duel. Following a stint working in the household of a Roman Catholic bishop, he served in the military and was involved in the 1571 naval battle of Lepanto against the Ottomans. He was given command of a skiff despite suffering from malaria at the time and received wounds that left him without the use of his left arm. Then, in 1575, he was captured by pirates and held to ransom for five years. Periods as a civil servant and tax collector followed, along with a number of short stays in prison over apparent financial irregularities. His first major literary work, *La Galatea*, appeared in 1585. It was only from the mid-1600s, once he had secured a wealthy patron – the Duke of Lamos – that he was able to afford to devote himself more fully to writing.

Given the nature of his own life, the episodic structure of *Don Quixote* perhaps came naturally to him. The book's central figure is Alonso Quixano, a lean, idealistic, middle-aged *hidalgo* – or low-ranking nobleman – from La Mancha. Having feasted on literary chivalric romances (in the process, depriving himself of sleep, drying out his brain and sending himself mad), Quixano determines to revive the traditions of those tales and become a knight-errant, travelling the land in search of adventure and good deeds to do. He rebrands himself as Don Quixote for the purpose and appoints Sancho Panza, a thick-set, plain-speaking, unsophisticated farmer, to serve as his squire. They embark on their adventures, one with his head in the clouds and the other with his feet firmly on the ground, quickly establishing the mismatched pair as one of the great double-acts of history.

Cervantes presents the book as being based on real sources – items in the La Mancha archive and a translation of an Arabic text. One of the great enduring themes of the work is the tension between truth and fiction. Among the myriad characters Quixote and Panza encounter – from priests and prostitutes to soldiers, goat-herds and criminals – several have narratives that contain events from the real world. By contrast, Quixote himself struggles to discern what is true and what is the product of his imagination. Donning a suit of armour and having nominated an unwitting local farmgirl as his true love, his dislocation from reality accelerates, not least when he imagines windmills to be ferocious giants. (This episode, in which he 'tilts' at the windmills – attacking them with his lance – gave us a whole new idiom.) As Quixote battles with the world he encounters, the reader is left to wonder how much an individual can command their own destiny through free will and to what extent they are subject to fate.

THE ORIGINAL LOTHARIO

Don Quixote gifted us a good number of words and phrases – not least, the adjective 'quixotic', meaning one who is idealistic and impractical. It is sometimes said that English dramatist Nicholas Rowe gave us the original Lothario – a bounder who acts selfishly in his sexual interactions with women – in his 1703 play, *The Fair Penitent*. However, it seems we might fairly credit this to Cervantes too. In a story related in the first volume of *Don Quixote*, 'The Man Who Was Recklessly Curious', a figure called Lothario is called upon to seduce his friend's wife in order to test her faithfulness. He may be an unwilling suitor but he surely has claim to be the original Lothario.

Quixote emerges from the first volume of the book as a hapless hero whose misjudgements and misfortunes result in all manner of calamity (with Panza frequently bearing the brunt). The second volume is a rather different beast, less joyously farcical but still concerned with the nature of reality. Published ten years after the first, volume two uses the dramatic conceit that Don Quixote is familiar with the fact that his story had been documented and widely read, and that a falsified 'second volume' is also in existence. This is meta-fiction early seventeenth-century style. After suffering assorted injuries and indignities, Quixote returns home and takes to what proves to be his deathbed. At the last, he regains his sanity and turns his back on his chivalric fantasy, shrugging off his identity as Don Quixote to become, once more, Alonso Quixano the Good.

In plundering and manipulating the form of the chivalric romance, Cervantes gave himself the tools to craft a new literary genre. One that brought multiple strands into a complex, unified narrative that speaks not only of events but of characters with complex psychologies and rich inner lives. He did the literary equivalent of a Renaissance artist, giving depth to his subjects where not so long before they had tended to serve rather as generic ciphers.

It is difficult to underestimate the literary influence of the work. To some extent, every novel since owes a debt to *Don Quixote* as the original trailblazer. It has been openly admired by a formidable number of other major authors, from Goethe and Flaubert to Dickens and Nabokov. Indeed, the novel is explicitly referenced in several major literary works, among them *The Adventures of Huckleberry Finn* (Mark Twain), *Cyrano de Bergerac* (Edmond Rostand) and *The Three Musketeers* (Alexandre Dumas).

Don Quixote is a work that itself challenges us as readers to examine the very nature of truth and virtue and to ponder how far we can mould our own lives. As such, it is a keystone of the Western literary canon. But as if that were not enough, Cervantes gifted us an entire literary form that has reached more people than any other in the centuries since he crafted his story.

TITLE: THE COMPLETE WORKS

AUTHOR: WILLIAM SHAKESPEARE
DATE: 1623

. . . .

Who could have guessed that the son of a moderately successful Elizabethan glove-maker from the English Midlands would become the great behemoth dominating the Western cultural landscape? But that has been the fate of William Shakespeare, a man of whom we know remarkably little other than the fact that he was the author of a body of literary work (at least 37 plays, 154 sonnets and a handful of longer poems) that is still read, enjoyed and analysed to within an inch of its life throughout the world to this day.

Of course, Shakespeare never set out to write a 'book' as such, and his works were published together, in a *First Folio*, only some seven years after his death. But in the four hundred years since his demise, he has been widely regarded as the single greatest and most important writer in the English language.

He is most celebrated for his plays, traditionally grouped into Tragedies, Comedies and Histories. There are several different reasons behind his ongoing impact. First, he was a supreme storyteller and creator of character. *Hamlet*, *Romeo and Juliet*, *King Lear*, *Macbeth*, *A Midsummer Night's Dream*, *Antony and Cleopatra*, *Henry V* ... the list, literally, goes on and on. To imagine a cultural landscape in which Shakespeare had never written is akin to thinking of the history of popular music without The Beatles. The world would be a lesser place without Shakespeare's work, even if over-familiarity with his *oeuvre* sometimes encourages it to be taken for granted.

Shakespeare also had the good fortune to write in the language that over the next few centuries would become the *lingua franca* for vast swathes of the planet, ensuring his work spread across the globe. But why did Shakespeare's name become supreme so widely, and not that of some other writer? Part of the answer is surely his preternatural ability to address themes of universality – love and hate, war, peace and power, freedom, revenge, greed, lust and more. Nelson Mandela, a man whose life seemingly had little in common with that of Shakespeare, was moved to observe: 'Shakespeare always seems to have something to say to us.' Ben Jonson, one of the writer's Elizabethan contemporaries, memorably described him as 'not of an age, but for all time'. His plays transcend time and place in a unique way. He himself seems to have had in mind that he was communicating to humanity in its entirety, his Globe Theatre bearing the motto *'Totus mundus agit histrionem'* ('The entire world is a playhouse').

In his characterization and plotting, Shakespeare explored archetypes, touchstone figures and ideas recognizable from theatrical tradition. But he added a layer of psychological complexity that pushed the expectations of what drama and literature can achieve. His archetypes became fully formed humans, imbued with the full gamut of emotions, strengths and frailties – all communicated in the most memorable of language. Has there ever been a more complete study of a man in crisis, for instance, than that of Hamlet? Or a single more memorable exploration of the human psyche than his 'To be or not to be' soliloquy? If one thinks of the defining narrative of doomed love, who – even today – need look further than Romeo and Juliet? If one is accusing another of treachery, still they are likely to reach for the words of Julius Caesar: 'Et tu, Brute?' For evidence of his brilliance as a purveyor of psychological depth, study the works of Sigmund Freud, written several centuries later. Freud littered his writings with quotations from the playwright, whom he described as 'the greatest of poets'.

EXPENSIVE WORDS

It is of course ridiculous to attempt to attribute a financial value to Shakespeare's works. However, the value placed upon the 1623 *First Folio* of his plays might at least hint at the esteem in which he is held. The print run of the *Folio* was around a thousand and retailed for a princely £1 in its year of publication. Some 235 copies remain in existence, of which fewer than 20 are complete and undamaged. A copy (printed after his death, remember, and lacking any physical connection to the author such as a signature) was auctioned in New York in 2020 for US$9.98 million. Not bad for a second-hand book!

Shakespeare's ability to communicate emotion and investigate complexity is intrinsically linked to his mastery of language – his ability to write lines unrivalled in their knack of sticking in the mind. *Hamlet* alone provides over two hundred quotations in the *Oxford Dictionary of Quotations*. The modern English speaker has a vocabulary of some ten to twenty thousand words, of which they will regularly use but a small proportion. Shakespeare employed just over twenty-nine thousand different words in his plays.

Moreover, he invented a vast number of new ones. Samuel Johnson attributed more words to him than any other writer in his first *Dictionary of the English Language*, and the current *Oxford English Dictionary* uses two thousand supporting quotations from the Bard. It seems fair to say that he was responsible for the generation of at least some seventeen hundred new words. A small selection includes: antipathy, arch-villain, assassination, barefaced, bedazzle, belongings, courtship, dauntless, dewdrop, employer, epileptic, equivocal, fairyland, fashionable, frugal, go-between, homely, honey-tongued, impartial, ladybird, lament, leapfrog, lustrous, nimble-footed, outbreak, pander, prodigious, puke, rant, schoolboy, silliness, time-honoured, unearthly, useful, vulnerable, watchdog, well-bred and zany.

His skill at coining new phrases also *beggars description* (a phrase he was the first to use in *Antony and Cleopatra*). To give just a very few examples, without Shakespeare we would not have dishes fit for the gods (*Julius Caesar*), blinking idiots (*The Merchant of Venice*), brave new worlds (*The Tempest*), towers of strength (*Richard III*) or wild-goose chases (*Romeo and Juliet*). And how less rich would the world be without concepts such as the seven ages of Man (*As You Like It*), the green-eyed monster (*Othello*) or the winter of our discontent (*Richard III*).

By exploring the boundaries of drama and verse, examining character in terms of psychological truth and expressing it all in the most astonishing language, Shakespeare changed history. Sometimes literally so – our understanding of the character of Richard III, for instance, arguably owes much more to the Bard's depiction of him than evidence in the historical record. But more importantly, he encourages us to ask what it really means to be human – a question he addressed so completely that his work is performed and inspires as much today as when it was first written.

TITLE: *DIALOGUE CONCERNING THE TWO CHIEF WORLD SYSTEMS*

AUTHOR: GALILEO GALILEI
DATE: 1632

. . . .

The Dialogue Concerning the Two Chief World Systems is a landmark scientific treatise that enabled the world's transition from one widely held view of itself to an entirely different one. It challenged the teachings of the Roman Catholic Church that, at the time, dominated much of European thought, and made the life of its author – the Italian astronomer, engineer and physicist, Galileo Galilei – very uncomfortable. But today no serious reader veers from its dominant idea that the Earth is not the centre of the Universe, but in fact the Earth and the other planets orbit the Sun.

The treatise builds on the work of the Polish-born Nicolaus Copernicus (1473–1543), especially his 1543 opus, *On the Revolutions of the Celestial Spheres*, which outlined a vision of the cosmos contrasting with the Ptolemaic system that puts our planet at the centre of everything – and which had dominated religious and scientific teaching since ancient times. It had immediately sparked the criticism of major religious figures, both Catholics and Reformists, who believed its radical thesis was at odds with scriptural teaching. For instance, Martin Luther is said to have noted: 'This fool wishes to reverse the entire science of astronomy; but sacred Scripture tells us [Joshua 10:13] that Joshua commanded the sun to stand still, and not the earth.'

Copernicus wrote in a style almost impenetrable to all but the most scientifically minded. With the religious establishment firmly set against him, his work failed to seep into the popular consciousness. Nonetheless, it did find wide readership among the scientific community (although reference to it was often caveated that it was a useful theoretical model, not one fixed in reality). It was also placed on the Catholic Church's Index of Forbidden Books in 1616, where it remained for over a hundred and forty years.

The Pisan-born Galileo had become convinced of Copernicus's ideas as a result of a raft of astronomical observations he made around 1609. He had then written to one of his students in 1613 about how Copernican theory might be reconciled with certain biblical passages, and the letter had brought him to the attention of the Inquisition in Rome. The Inquisition concluded that Copernican heliocentrism was heretical, not to mention 'foolish and absurd', and Galileo was warned to cease its promotion. But when Pope Urban VIII took over at the Vatican in 1623, Galileo found himself with an unexpected friend – one who gave his blessing to Galileo to write an exploration of heliocentrism as long as he didn't come out for its adoption.

BANNED!

The Roman Catholic Church introduced its *Index Librorum Prohibitorum* ('List of Prohibited Books') in the first half of the sixteenth century, just as developments in printing technology were creating a new, much bigger audience for literary material. The list would go on to include all manner of works, from fiction and philosophy to scientific papers and unapproved versions of the Bible. Thousands of books came to be blacklisted for their potential to be 'disruptive' to the Church and wider society. It was only in 1966 that the *Index* was formally done away with during the tenure of Pope Paul VI – a mere five years after Simone de Beauvoir's *The Second Sex* became one of the last modern classics to fall foul of the censors.

The result was *The Dialogue*, published in 1632 with the assent of the Inquisition. The book is structured as a conversation held over several days between two philosophers – Salviati, who argues Copernicus's corner, and Simplicio, who stands with the Ptolemaic worldview – and a neutral layman, Sagredo. They debate the various merits of each side, frequently through the use of thought experiments. For instance, if the earth is in motion, should not a cannon-ball fired in one direction land further away than if fired in the opposite direction?

While Galileo aimed for a neutral tone, and declared the subject matter of the book as 'hypothetical', it was quite apparent to most observers what side of the argument he was on. Nor did it help that Simplicio – a name that conjures up the very notion of a 'simpleton' – is frequently the subject of ridicule. When Galileo finished the book in 1630, it was due to go before the censors in Rome and would not likely have passed them unamended. But because of an outbreak of the plague, he was allowed to send it to the censors in Florence instead, who proved a rather easier audience.

Yet he would not get an easy ride for long, not least because Urban VIII felt offended at having his side of the argument represented by a figure such as Simplicio. In 1633 Galileo was brought before the Inquisition in Rome, who reminded him of the earlier admonition to abandon Copernican theory. Galileo claimed he had only discussed the theory, not defended it, before agreeing that he was guilty of 'overstating his case'. Judged 'vehemently suspect of heresy', he was forced to renounce his troublesome beliefs and the book itself was banned. Galileo was sentenced to imprisonment at the Inquisition's pleasure, although in reality he was held under house-arrest (first at a friend's palace in Siena and then in a villa in the Tuscan countryside) for the rest of his life. As his punishment was handed down, legend has it that Galileo repeated under his breath, 'And yet it moves', although the story is probably apocryphal.

Galileo was a giant of the scientific world on many counts – a pioneer of the scientific method, who brought together mathematics and theoretical and experimental physics to tackle age-old mysteries. After his altercations with the Vatican, he understandably largely steered clear of the subject of heliocentrism. It was only in the eighteenth century that the Church allowed the publication of *The Dialogue* and only in 1835 that it was formally removed from the *Index* in all its forms. But by then, Galileo had all but won the argument. The world had come to realize that our little planet is not, after all, the centre of everything. And despite that, the earth literally carries on turning. Speaking in 1939, Pope Pius XII even called Galileo one of the 'most audacious heroes of research ... not afraid of the stumbling blocks and the risks on the way, nor fearful of the funereal monuments'. True, and an acknowledgement better late than never.

TITLE: *PRINCIPIA*

AUTHOR: ISAAC NEWTON
DATE: 1687

. . . .

Philosophiæ Naturalis Principia Mathematica (*Mathematical Principles of Natural Philosophy*; often abbreviated to simply the *Principia*) is a three-volume work that introduced Isaac Newton's law of universal gravitation and his three laws of motion. It became a lynchpin for the entirety of modern scientific thought and has remained a staple text, even after Einstein's *General Theory of Relativity* and the emergence of quantum mechanics undermined its claims to universality.

Born in Lincolnshire, England, in 1642, Newton was one of the most formidable polymaths of his day, making numerous notable contributions across a range of fields. He was a key figure, for instance, in the development of telescopic lenses, laid the framework for infinitesimal calculus and even spent a significant amount of time on alchemical studies. But it was the *Principia* that raised his name into the echelons of the truly great scientific thinkers.

In his elucidation of his three laws of motion, he became the first to comprehensively account for the movement of objects through space using theoretical mathematics. The first of these laws is the law of inertia, which states: 'An object at rest will remain at rest unless acted on by an unbalanced force. An object in motion continues in motion with the same speed and in the same direction unless acted upon by an unbalanced force.' His second law establishes that acceleration is produced when a force acts on a mass. The larger the mass, the larger the force required to accelerate it. His third law, meanwhile, says that for every action, there is an equal but opposite reaction. With a few strokes of his quill (he wrote his text in Latin, as was customary for academic texts at the time), Newton thus established the foundations of modern mechanics.

GRAPPLE WITH AN APPLE

The quasi-legendary status of the circumstances of Newton's gravitational revelations in the *Principia* was famously encapsulated by Lord Byron, who wrote in *Don Juan*: 'When Newton saw an apple fall, he found / In that slight startle from his contemplation ... / A mode of proving that the earth turn'd round / In a most natural whirl, called "gravitation".' Byron also proved himself something of a prophesier in the verse, when he predicted that the discoveries of Newton – 'the sole mortal who could grapple, / Since Adam – with a fall – or with an apple' – would 'full soon' see steam-engines conduct man to the moon!

Yet, arguably, his theory of universal gravitation had an even greater impact. Fundamentally, it sought to show that all things are attracted to all other things in space by virtue of an invisible force. It describes how any two masses attract each other with a force equal to a constant (the gravitational constant) multiplied by the product of the two masses and divided by the square of the distance between them.

Quite how he arrived at this insight is a mystery shrouded in legend. One popular version of the circumstances is that it came to him as he sat beneath a tree and an apple fell on his head. But it is now largely accepted that the story, though greatly appealing, is apocryphal. Nonetheless, it is by no means beyond the realms of possibility that he was at least in part driven towards his startling conclusion by witnessing a similar scenario. Seeing an apple being 'pulled' from a tree towards the earth, he might well have pondered why it always took the route downwards to the earth and did not, say, fly upwards into space or in some other direction altogether.

Regardless of how he arrived at it, the theory at last explained why things move as they do – on earth and in space. Among other things, it provided the longed-for mathematical proof of the veracity of Copernicus's heliocentric model. In devising his thesis, Newton also made plentiful use of Johannes Kepler's planetary observations. As Newton would memorably put it: 'If I have seen further, it is by standing on the shoulders of giants.' Yet, he was under no illusion that he had hit upon a 'theory of everything'. 'Gravity explains the motions of the planets,' he observed, 'but it cannot explain who set the planets in motion.'

The *Principia* emerged from a much shorter paper, '*De Motu*' ('On Motion'), that Newton composed in 1684 after the astronomer Edmond Halley asked for his help in solving some problems of orbital dynamics. While the kernels of the three laws of motion were contained within it, it did not however address the subject of universal gravitation. But once the *Principia* emerged, Newton was elevated to superstar status in the scientific firmament.

Lucrative public offices came his way, as did a knighthood. But there would be controversies too. In particular, he ended up in an unseemly spat with the German philosopher and mathematician, Gottfried Wilhelm Leibniz, over which of them was the inventor of calculus. Both men spent years developing their systems, although Leibniz was the first to go public with his discoveries. It is now widely agreed that Newton had in fact developed his calculus earlier than the German, but that both arrived at their results entirely independently. Not even Leibniz's death in 1716 could snuff out the bad blood. The affair would hover in the background of everything Newton did until his own death in 1726.

It is *Principia*, though, that stands as his masterpiece and secures Newton the place in history that he craved. Alexander Pope wrote him a moving epitaph: 'Nature and nature's laws lay hid in night; / God said "Let Newton be" and all was light.' More than two hundred years later, Albert Einstein – the man whose own work forced a fundamental reconsideration of *Principia* – confirmed his enduring legacy: 'Newton's age has long since passed through the sieve of oblivion, the doubtful striving and suffering of his generation has vanished from our ken; the works of some few great thinkers and artists have remained, to delight and ennoble those who come after us. Newton's discoveries have passed into the stock of accepted knowledge.'

TITLE: *ON THE SOCIAL CONTRACT; OR, PRINCIPLES OF POLITICAL RIGHT*

AUTHOR: JEAN-JACQUES ROUSSEAU

DATE: 1742

. . . .

The Social Contract was a revolutionary book in the truest sense of the word, firing the imaginations and the passions of the leading lights of the French Revolution – an epoch-defining event that Rousseau did not witness, having died a decade or so before it started, but of which he was a posthumous figurehead. One of Rousseau's greatest champions was Maximilien Robespierre, who wrote of him in his diary: 'Divine man! It was you who taught me to know myself. When I was young you brought me to appreciate the true dignity of my nature and to reflect on the great principles which govern the social order.'

Rousseau was born in Geneva in 1712 and proved to be almost as talented a musician and composer as he was a philosopher. One of his early achievements was the development of a system of mathematical musical notation. After dividing his time between various continental cities, he came to Paris when he was about thirty years old and soon became a fixture in its cultural and philosophical scene. Paris was his spiritual home, and where his philosophy would find its most ardent audience.

He struck up a particular friendship with Denis Diderot, the celebrated Enlightenment philosopher and editor of the famous *Encyclopaedia, or a Systematic Dictionary of the Sciences, Arts, and Crafts*. Rousseau's own career as a philosopher began in earnest when he won an essay-writing competition in 1750 on the subject of the moral benefits of the arts and sciences. He developed some of the themes from that paper in what became his first major work, *Discourse on the Origin and Basis of Inequality Among Men* (also known as the *Second Discourse*), published in 1754. There he reflected on what he considered to be humankind's 'state of nature'. He concluded that Man in his primitive state was a figure whose morals had not yet been corrupted and who showed a gentleness 'when placed by nature at an equal distance from the stupidity of brutes and the fatal enlightenment of civil man'.

Primitive man, according to Rousseau, occupied a happy middle ground between brutish creatures and the decadent modern Man in his civil society. Civil society, he contended, was not a driver of progress but rather of human decay. If that were not critical enough, he also identified private property as the cause of its deep inequality:

The first man who, having fenced in a piece of
land, said 'This is mine', and found people naïve
enough to believe him, that man was the true
founder of civil society. From how many crimes,
wars, and murders, from how many horrors
and misfortunes might not any one have saved
mankind, by pulling up the stakes, or filling
up the ditch, and crying to his fellows: Beware
of listening to this impostor; you are undone
if you once forget that the fruits of the earth
belong to us all, and the earth itself to nobody.

The revolutionary potential of such discourse was obvious
and caused many in authority to regard Rousseau as a
dangerous renegade. More controversy followed in 1762
with *Emile, or On Education*, with its confrontational
assertion: 'Everything is good as it leaves the hands of the
Author of things; everything degenerates in the hands of
man.' Rousseau's rebuttal of certain basic Christian tenets
and his demand for complete religious tolerance saw the
book banned in Paris and Geneva. But it was *The Social
Contract*, published the same year, that really rocked the boat.

Rousseau argued that civil society denigrates humanity, a
position he framed in one of philosophy's most memorable
quotations: 'Man is born free, and everywhere he is in
chains. Those who think themselves the masters of others
are indeed greater slaves than they.' He would go on to make
the case against the divine right of monarchs and argued
that no country had the right to impose its rule on another

('Let us then admit that force does not create right, and that we are obliged to obey only legitimate powers').

CONFESSIONS

Rousseau composed several volumes of memoir that were published after his death under the title *Confessions*. The work is regarded as one of the first autobiographies in a truly modern sense, one of the earliest examples of an introspective study of one's own life by a non-religious figure. The book is notable too for recounting an anecdote about 'a great princess' who, when told that the peasants had no bread, replied: 'Then let them eat brioches.' This was the source of the saying so often later attributed to Marie-Antoinette, appearing a full seven years before she was alleged to have damagingly coined the phrase.

Sovereign power should reside with the people (including women – another radical position for the time), with all citizens participating in government. Harking back to a model of pure democracy, Rousseau called for a society in which all are equal and where laws are made in accordance with the common will, which he said would naturally promote justice and egalitarianism. He furthermore contended that the government should be distinct from this popular legislature, executing its business but under threat of abolition should it act against the will of the people.

Unsurprisingly, Europe's powers by now considered him entirely beyond the pale and he spent the next few years traversing the continent in search of asylum. He died in 1778 but his time was still to come. A hero of the French Revolution, one wonders what he would have made of, say, Robespierre's Reign of Terror. Regardless, in 1794, sixteen years after his death, he was interred in the Panthéon in Paris, commemorated as a national hero. Writing in the twentieth century, American philosopher Will Durant said of him:

> How did it come about that this man, after his death, triumphed over Voltaire, revived religion, transformed education, elevated the morals of France, inspired the Romantic movement and the French Revolution, influenced the philosophy of Kant and Schopenhauer, the plays of Schiller, the novels of Goethe, the poems of Wordsworth, Byron, and Shelley, the socialism of Marx, the ethics of Tolstoy, and, altogether, had more effect upon posterity than any other writer or thinker of that eighteenth century in which writers were more influential than they had ever been before?

TITLE: *A DICTIONARY OF THE ENGLISH LANGUAGE*

AUTHOR: SAMUEL JOHNSON

DATE: 1755

. . . .

In the summer of 1746, a group of booksellers, publishers and printers in London – among them, Thomas Longman, founder of the eponymous publishing house that continues to thrive today – reached the conclusion that they needed to commission a comprehensive dictionary of the English language. It resulted in one of the landmark publications in literary history – one that changed perceptions of what language is and how we think about it.

The world of reading changed much in eighteenth-century Britain. Literacy levels were on the rise and the costs of producing books, newspapers, pamphlets and the like led to a surge in demand for the written word. Ever larger numbers of people could now obtain reading materials at a reasonable price. But the more that was printed, the more it became obvious that the English language was an amalgam. A language that had evolved in many beautiful ways over many centuries, it lacked hard-and-fast rules.

That might have been OK when the written word was the concern of a relative few – the rich and the professionally religious – as had been the way until not long before. But now it was in the hands of the masses, there was a demand for greater clarity. How should words be spelled? Even more fundamentally, what meaning, or range of meanings, does each individual word possess? And how should they be used and understood in terms of a grammatical framework?

That group of publishing professionals who met in 1746 knew that the project of aggregating all the words in the language and bringing some order to them was vast. There were already dictionaries out there but they were of varying quality, frequently unreliable, often highly eccentric (several were arranged thematically rather than alphabetically, which did not help clarity) and none could claim to be definitive. Some were little more than word lists. What was needed was something authoritative.

Longman and his companions decide to approach Samuel Johnson, a much-respected writer – a journalist, poet, playwright, biographer and critic. They offered him 1,500 guineas (somewhere in the region of £250,000 today) to take on the job. He told them it would take him three years. In the event, it took him nearer nine, but even that seems swift given the scale of the challenge.

He undertook the work at his home at 17 Gough Square, London, spending the first year crafting a plan detailing his aspirations for the book and his proposed methodology. The project was his alone to an extraordinary extent. He employed a few staff to assist him, but this was almost exclusively restricted to administrative support. Almost single-handedly, he was charged with taking the language and shaking it into some sort of order. As his patron, the Earl of Chesterfield, put it: 'We must have recourse to the old Roman expedient in times of confusion, and choose a dictator. Upon this principle, I give my vote for Mr Johnson to fill that great and arduous post.'

What made the *Dictionary* unique was Johnson's decision to provide not only accurate definitions for every word, but also quotations to illustrate these definitions. In a remarkable feat of scholarliness, he sourced these quotes from writers across the ages. It is true that he favoured some more than others. William Shakespeare, John Milton, John Dryden, Alexander Pope and Edmund Spenser all feature heavily. But the breadth of his reading is almost unfathomable. (Johnson was infamous for marking his books with copious notes and comments.)

WHAT DO YOU MEAN?

Johnson was not above having some fun with his definitions. He could be variously wry, self-effacing and acerbic. A 'lexicographer' he defined as 'a writer of dictionaries; a harmless drudge that busies himself in tracing the original and detailing the signification of words'. 'Excise', meanwhile, is 'a hateful tax levied upon commodities and adjudged not by the common judges of property but wretches hired by those to whom excise is paid'. And there was a particularly pointed definition for Philip Stanhope, the Earl of Chesterfield – his patron, with whom he had a somewhat difficult relationship. Johnson defined a 'patron' as 'one who countenances, supports, or protects. Commonly a wretch who supports with insolence, and is paid with flattery.' Ouch!

In 1755, the complete first edition went on sale, with some 43,000 words defined and illustrated by 114,000 quotations. Self-described on its front page, here was *A DICTIONARY of the ENGLISH LANGUAGE: in which The WORDS are deduced from their ORIGINALS, and ILLUSTRATED in their*

DIFFERENT SIGNIFICATIONS by EXAMPLES from the best WRITERS. To which are prefixed, A HISTORY of the LANGUAGE, and AN ENGLISH GRAMMAR. By SAMUEL JOHNSON, A.M. In TWO Volumes.

In the preface, Johnson talked of finding the language 'copious without order, and energetick without rules', with 'perplexity to be disentangled, and confusion to be regulated'. Yet his years as a lexicographer had also taught him that language cannot be entirely tamed and nor should it. It changes and evolves and, he came to understand, it was not his job to make it 'correct' but rather to record it in its present state as best he could. The lexicographer as reporter, not embalmer.

The *Dictionary* itself was a beautiful artefact, printed on giant sheets of the finest paper. The cost was prohibitive for most. In its first thirty years of existence, sales did not exceed ten thousand copies. Yet its importance was recognized almost from the outset.

James Boswell, in his *Life of Samuel Johnson*, would write that 'the world contemplated with wonder so stupendous a work achieved by one man, while other countries had thought such undertakings fit only for whole academies'. (The politician and writer Horace Walpole was rather more mealy-mouthed in declaring that Johnson's reputation would not be 'very lasting' and that the task of compiling the dictionary had proven 'too much for one man'.)

Johnson's dictionary is not without its idiosyncrasies and even failings. The author's personality and prejudices sometimes obtrude through – he gave short shrift to certain words rooted in French, one or two words were missed out altogether and he was adamant that no word in the English language began with 'X'. Nonetheless, it set the standard for all other dictionaries, and had no rival in English until the appearance of the *Oxford English Dictionary* a century and a half later. Notably, the *OED* incorporated almost two thousand of his definitions without any substantial change.

The *Dictionary* quickly became a cultural treasure, not merely a guide to the English language but a celebration of the power of the word and an exploration of art and society. Its impact is measurable in practical terms too. For instance, the US Courts have routinely turned to Johnson's dictionary over the centuries when it has come to examining the wording – the meaning – of founding documents such as the Constitution. It is also notable that Johnson produced several revised editions of the *Dictionary* over the remainder of his life but so complete was his first attempt that very few additional words were added.

It is not too much to say that in his defining of words, Johnson redefined our understanding of what it is to communicate as humans. According to Walter Jackson Bate, a twentieth-century biographer of Johnson, the *Dictionary* 'easily ranks as one of the greatest single achievements of scholarship, and probably the greatest ever performed by one individual ...'

TITLE: *COMMON SENSE*

AUTHOR: THOMAS PAINE
DATE: 1776

. . . .

Published in January 1776 in Philadelphia, the largest city in the then American colony of Pennsylvania, *Common Sense* was a cutting forty-seven-page pamphlet raging against the inequities of royal rule. In a few short months, it became one of the drivers of the American War of Independence that saw the overthrow of British rule and the establishment of the United States of America. At a moment when many of those who decried British rule eschewed the idea of a complete break, Paine gave wings to that very idea.

Paine was born in the English county of Norfolk in 1737 and had left school when he was thirteen to help out at his father's corset shop. When he was twenty, he briefly served as crew on a privateer, then had some unsuccessful attempts at starting his own business before finding work as a tax collector for the government – a job from which he was ultimately fired, and which left him with a low opinion of the British government.

With little going for him professionally, he decided to start anew in 1774 and so set out for America. In London, he had met Benjamin Franklin, one of the most influential Americans of the age, and persuaded him to furnish him with a letter of recommendation. As a result, when he arrived in Philadelphia, Paine was able to find work as a journalist, having earned himself a reputation back in Britain as a talented pamphleteer.

He found America simmering with discontent at the heavy hand of the British government – a position with which he had much sympathy. The Americans considered themselves to be over-taxed and shackled by British trade restrictions. The year before his arrival had seen the famous Boston Tea Party, when a tea shipment was cast into Boston harbour in protest against the favourable terms under which the British East India Company was permitted to operate, and because many of the colonists refused the idea of taxation by an administration in which they were not permitted representation.

There was a growing feeling that the Anglo-American relationship needed major revision. But fewer were convinced that a complete divorce was the answer. Then Paine published his pamphlet in the early part of January 1776, signing it only 'by an Englishman'. Franklin and another of the 'Founding Fathers', Benjamin Rush, encouraged him in the project, and Paine duly took no prisoners.

Where others saved their fiercest criticism for the British government and parliament, Paine directed his complaints towards the monarch himself, George III. The idea of hereditary monarchy, he suggested, was utterly absurd, and Europe's numerous failing monarchies provided ample evidence of it. Why should the colonist seek rapprochement with a regime intent on imposing unfair taxes and unjust laws? Hadn't most of the colonists fled to escape all that in the first place anyway?

'Europe, and not England, is the parent country of America,' he wrote. 'This new world hath been the asylum for the persecuted lovers of civil and religious liberty from every part of Europe. Hither they have fled, not from the tender embraces of the mother, but from the cruelty of the monster; and it is so far true of England, that the same tyranny which drove the first emigrants from home, pursues their descendants still.' Time to break away, he contended: 'We have every opportunity and every encouragement before us, to form the noblest purest constitution on the face of the earth. We have it in our power to begin the world over again.' A world, for instance, where property ownership was not a prerequisite to having a vote or holding public office.

It was incendiary, certainly. Too much, even, for some of the most prominent of the American would-be revolutionaries. But Paine's words quickly found a mass audience. The pamphlet is estimated to have sold over five hundred thousand copies during the course of the American War of Independence and found a much wider audience through black market reproductions and public readings in pubs and meeting halls.

Paine had wanted to call the work *The Plain Truth* but Rush persuaded him to go with *Common Sense*, judging that the title better reflected one of Paine's major concerns: that ordinary people ought to trust their feelings rather than become immersed in abstract political debate. One could debate all day the rights and wrongs of breaking with the mother country, but why stay when that country mistreats you, he suggested. 'Of more worth is one honest man to society and in the sight of God, than all the crowned ruffians that ever lived.' And now was the colonies' moment, 'that peculiar time, which never happens to a nation but once'.

Thomas Jefferson is said to have considered Paine the pre-eminent writer of Revolutionary America, a man who could find the voice and language to truly connect with a mass audience. The future second president of the USA, John Adams, was another who recognized his impact, writing to his wife in April 1776: '*Common Sense*, like a ray of revelation, has come in seasonably to clear our doubts, and to fix our choice.' Nonetheless, Adams was also among those wary of the pamphlet's arguments, some of which he addressed in his own tract of the same year, *Thoughts on Government*.

KNOW YOUR RIGHTS

Paine would go on to author another major tract in 1791, *Rights of Man*, which argued in defence of another revolution – this time, the one then overtaking France. It was written in response to Edmund Burke's attack on the revolution, *Reflections on the Revolution in France*, written the previous year. The British government was concerned that Paine's views would find an audience at home and so a writ was issued for his arrest in 1792. Having returned from America, Paine fled to France, becoming immersed in the fervid political scene there until he was arrested in Paris in late 1793, winning his freedom only after the intervention of an old American ally (and another future US president), James Monroe. Tried in absentia in Britain, he was convicted of seditious libel against Burke but avoided punishment by never returning to his native country.

Regardless of his detractors, Paine's voice proved perhaps, in the moment, the most influential of the many competing to steer the direction of events at that pivotal time. The American colonies did make that break with the colonial power, just as he suggested. His writings achieved permanent impact as a formative influence on both the US Constitution and the Bill of Rights. As such, Paine stands as one of the great Enlightenment champions of civil and human rights.

TITLE: *THE WEALTH OF NATIONS*

AUTHOR: ADAM SMITH
DATE: 1776

. . . .

An Inquiry into the Nature and Causes of the Wealth of Nations (to give it its full title) was published in the same year that the American colonies declared their independence from Britain. It was a fitting coincidence, given that Adam Smith's landmark work has come to be regarded as the foundation text of classical economics – a blueprint for the sort of free market economic model upon which the US based its rise to global dominance. Almost single-handedly, Smith created economics as a heavyweight academic discipline, and established the free market as the system of choice for nations across the globe.

Smith was born in Kirkcaldy, Scotland, in 1723 and studied moral philosophy at the University of Glasgow before spending several years at the University of Oxford. Greatly influenced by Enlightenment philosophy, his own worldview was informed by his belief in the principles of liberty, reason and free speech. After winning good public notices for a series of lectures he delivered in Edinburgh in the 1750s, he became a professor at the University of Glasgow. Specializing in the fields of logic and moral philosophy, he struck up a notable friendship with his fellow Scottish philosopher, David Hume. Then, in 1764, Smith moved to France where he became acquainted with Voltaire and began to work on what would become his *magnum opus*, *The Wealth of Nations* – a book whose influence extended far beyond its author's death in 1790.

MY SECOND-BEST BOOK

While *The Wealth of Nations* is the book that ensured Smith's reputation as a great thinker, he is believed to have considered it inferior to his *Theory of Moral Sentiments*, published seventeen years earlier in 1759. A study of moral philosophy and conscience, he sought to understand from what source Man derives moral judgement. In concluding that it stems from our innately social and sympathetic nature, it has prompted many critics to suggest that the book is in stark contrast with his later, more celebrated work and its promotion of self-interest.

Published in two volumes, it was a revolutionary work in several respects. Primarily, it challenged the then prevailing orthodoxy of mercantilism, which argued that government intervention was necessary to maintain economic equilibrium. Under mercantilist thought, for instance, world trade was governed by the competing protectionist policies of different countries. Smith, though, argued that all nations would benefit from the wholesale removal of such protectionism.

These ideas required some fundamental intellectual adjustments. From time immemorial, the wealth of a nation had been thought of in terms of how much it possessed of whatever particular commodity it used as a store of wealth – typically gold or silver. But Smith argued that wealth was rather better measured by looking at the volume of all the goods and services that were traded by the population as a whole. A strongroom full of coinage in the royal palace means little if nobody has food to eat or clothes to wear or a public house to relax in. 'The annual labour of every nation is the fund which originally supplies it with all the necessaries and conveniences of life which it annually consumes,' Smith wrote. In effect, he was introducing the concept of Gross Domestic Product (GDP), which has become the standard – if itself imperfect – measure of a country's economic wellbeing.

That being established, Smith then made what at the time was a very bold claim: that this flow of goods and services is best encouraged not by the intervention of the government, but by non-intervention. By imposing tariffs or granting subsidies, he said, the natural flow of trade is skewed.

Prices become artificially set and all actors, especially the poor, suffer. But by allowing genuine competition between suppliers in a free market, those goods and services most wanted and needed by the largest number of consumers will be provided. This is not the result of suppliers' goodwill towards the consumer, but because the supplier's own self-interested wish for profit impels them to provide what the market demands. Equally, the self-interest of consumers compels them to buy from suppliers irrespective of any personal connection to them. In Smith's own words:

> Every individual necessarily labours to render the annual revenue of the society as great as he can. Generally, indeed, neither intends to promote the public interest, nor knows how much he is promoting it ... by directing that industry in such a manner as its produce may be of the greatest value, he intends only his own gain, and he is in this, as in many other cases, led by an invisible hand to promote an end which was no part of his intention.

he famously described the unseen force that makes free markets function as the 'invisible hand'. However, he did not believe that there was no role for government at all. Rather, it should play only a limited role under certain conditions. For example, he was sceptical that the free market was well placed to provide in the areas of health and education – sectors that are essential to the proper functioning of society but that are not subject to the same rules of self-interested supply and demand that govern, for example, consumer products. Smith – recognizing the perils of unfettered greed – also advocated for taxation to deter consumers from improper or overly indulgent conduct. He also believed that the state ought to enforce the laws that protect private property in order to create the secure environment necessary for the free market to prosper.

Much of what he discussed has since become economic orthodoxy. He persuaded a vast swathe of the world that its interests are best served not by interfering in economic matters but by letting self-interest do the hard work. Of course, not everyone agreed – not least Karl Marx, who saw the pitfalls of the free market where Smith saw its advantages. But William Ewart Gladstone, Britain's four-time Liberal prime minister, was convinced, saying of Smith in 1890 that he was 'the man who first taught us that in our intercourse with other nations, as well as among ourselves, it was better to have our hands free than to have our hands and arms in manacles – who taught the great doctrines of Free Trade, and who has imbued the world with these doctrines'.

IV

THE NINETEENTH CENTURY

TITLE: *FAUST*

AUTHOR: JOHANN WOLFGANG VON GOETHE
DATE: 1808/1832

. . . .

Faust, a tragic drama in two parts, is considered by many the greatest literary work in the German language. Written by Johann Wolfgang von Goethe over a period of some sixty years, it examines what compromises the main protagonist is prepared to make in search of earthly satisfaction. As such, it has become something of a universal allegory; in essence, an exploration of the question proffered in the Gospel of Matthew (16:26): 'What good will it be for a man if he gains the whole world, yet forfeits his soul?'

Part One of *Faust* begins with a wager between God and the demon Mephistopheles. The latter claims he can lead astray the virtuous Faust, a man intent on understanding all that there is to know. Faust is himself growing increasingly frustrated by what he considers his lack of success in his quest. In fact, he is considering suicide when the sound of church bells persuades him out of his plan. He takes a walk into town, where he encounters a poodle that follows him home, where its true identity is revealed as Mephistopheles. The pair then make their fateful pact. If Mephistopheles can meet Faust's earthly desires so that he reaches a point where he wishes to remain in the moment and no longer feels compelled to strive further, then the demon can have his soul.

Among the favours Mephistopheles bestows, he helps Faust woo a neighbour to whom he is attracted, Gretchen (also known as Margaret), by bewitching her. But the relationship (if that is what it may be called) is ill-starred, resulting in the death of Gretchen's mother, her brother and her illegitimate newborn child (whom she drowns, leading to her conviction for murder). Faust, with the demon's help, attempts to free her from prison, but by now Gretchen can see him for what he truly is and refuses, offering herself up for the judgement of God instead.

Part Two is a rather different entity, in which Faust is whisked off to disparate settings across time in a series of more disjointed adventures. In search of the contentment he seeks, he variously takes in the court of the Holy Roman Emperor and visits Ancient Greece (where he woos Helen of Troy), before fighting in a war for the emperor and then building a commercial empire. When death arrives in old age, Faust remains disillusioned with the world but finds some form of heavenly salvation in respect of his unstinting striving after truth and knowledge and his unshakable belief that there exists something more elevated than himself.

The legend of Faust gained a cultural foothold in the sixteenth century – the story of a man who sells his soul to the devil in return for knowledge and pleasure during his life on earth. The true-life inspiration for the tale is often considered to be Johann Georg Faust, a German alchemist, astrologer and necromancer whose life spanned the late fifteenth and early sixteenth centuries. He was reputed to have died around 1540 when an alchemical experiment caused an explosion that rendered his body terribly mutilated. The Elizabethan playwright Christopher Marlowe gave the story wider currency with his version of the legend, *The Tragical History of the Life and Death of Doctor Faustus*.

MEET ME AT THE CROSSROADS

One of the more curious Faustian legends attached itself to Robert Johnson, a great Blues musician who died in 1938 when just twenty-seven years old. The story goes that the young Robert, who lived on a Mississippi plantation, yearned to be a virtuoso guitarist. He received instructions to take his guitar to a local crossroads one night, where he was met by the devil in human form, who tuned his guitar before returning it to Robert. After this diabolical intervention, Robert was recognized as a master player until his death, of uncertain causes, a few years later. Old yarn as it might be, it is proof of our enduring fascination with the Faustian myth.

Goethe was labouring on an early form of the work (called *Urfaust*, the original manuscript now lost) as early as 1772 but 'Part One' in the version we know today would not see publication until 1808. 'Part Two' appeared only in 1832, a full year after its author's death. Those timescales give some sense of the magnitude of the project. Its structural demands (much of the play is written in poetical forms) and the sheer range of its cultural, religious, historical and philosophical allusions ensured that it demanded all Goethe's energies.

The durability of the legend (and especially Goethe's version) is reflected in the vast number of cultural works it has inspired, from literary works and opera to ballet and the visual arts. The existential dilemma that Faust faces is timeless and universal, yet the play is sufficiently multifaceted that it takes on particular resonances under differing historical circumstances. It may be seen in the context of Goethe's own time, when tensions abounded between the Christian Church in Europe and the Enlightenment philosophy. It is fair to say that there are echoes of Faust, with his belief in action and the 'will to power', in the works of Friedrich Nietzsche too. But by 1936, Klaus Mann had reworked the story in his novel, *Mephisto*, to fit a world moulded by the rise of fascism. Meanwhile, Stephen Vincent Benét adapted the tale for his *The Devil and Daniel Webster* (1936), written against the backdrop of the Great Depression. As the existentialist philosopher Søren Kierkegaard noted: 'Every notable historical era will have its own Faust.'

The Faustian pact continues to resonate. If climate change is the single greatest challenge of our age, we might say there is something Faustian in the conflict between our yearning for the planet's ongoing wellbeing and our drive to satisfy our desires through the very consumption that endangers the planet. What are we prepared to sacrifice in order to get what we think we want? By confronting such questions, we are forced to evaluate what really matters to us and, in the process, perhaps gain a more complete understanding of who we are and, indeed, why we are. Goethe's *Faust* seems ultimately to tell us that our best hope is to always strive with purpose.

TITLE: 'THE MURDERS IN THE RUE MORGUE'

AUTHOR: EDGAR ALLAN POE
DATE: 1841

. . . .

'The Murders in the Rue Morgue' is only a short story, first published in the American *Graham's Magazine*, where its author worked at the time as an editor. Yet its influence belies its brevity. Not only did it spawn a new literary genre, detective fiction, that changed the world's literary culture, but it reflected the growing concern of the Victorian world to confront and overcome the 'social illness' of criminality that haunted the popular psyche. In a post-Enlightenment world, the literary detective (of which Poe's Dupin was the first great example) came to represent the triumph of reason, bringing order to a disordered world.

   C. Auguste Dupin, the hero of the story, is an amateur sleuth. At the start of the narrative, he and the unnamed narrator learn from the newspaper about a strange double-murder in their native Paris. The victims, Mme. L'Espanaye and her daughter, have been discovered at their property on the Rue Morgue. The mother has suffered terrible injuries, including multiple fractures and a neck wound that severs her head. The daughter, meanwhile, is found strangled and stuffed down a chimney. Stranger still, the killings were apparently committed in a locked fourth-floor room. Inside the room is a razor, a quantity of grey hair and some gold coins. Eyewitnesses report having heard two voices, one French and the other speaking a language they cannot recognize. Through a process of ratiocination – an exacting form of reasoning based on close observation – Dupin manages to solve the case and identify the extraordinary culprit.

Poe was born in Boston in 1809 and emerged as one of the nation's most significant writers, working across formats and genres. An established critic and poet and arguably the greatest short-story writer of his day, he was a pioneer of science fiction and a leading exponent of American Romanticism and the Gothic. Yet nothing outshone the success he enjoyed with Dupin, not only in 'The Murders in the Rue Morgue' but also in 'The Mystery of Marie Rogêt' and 'The Purloined Letter'. It was the latter of these that Poe considered 'perhaps the best of my tales of ratiocination' but it was the first story, which was originally to have been called 'Murders in the Rue Trianon', that laid down the blueprint. Yet Poe never saw great financial rewards for his publishing success. He was paid an additional $56 by the magazine that already employed him for the rights to 'The Murders in the Rue Morgue' – a figure that admittedly dwarfed the paltry $9 he received on publication of his poetic masterpiece, 'The Raven'.

The arrival of the first great literary detective had been a long time coming. One can see echoes of Dupin in, for example, the logical deductions of Voltaire's Zadig back in 1747, although the latter's intellectual feats were not directed towards solving crime but to addressing problems of philosophy. What crime writing did exist was epitomized by the sort of gory, melodramatic accounts of true-life crimes in publications like London's *Newgate Calendar*, a monthly account produced by the keeper of Newgate Prison. The *Calendar* would in turn inspire the Newgate novels of the 1820s–40s that retold the histories of various criminals of the past.

William Godwin published *Caleb Williams* in 1794, with the main protagonist solving a crime but not through a process of intellectual detection. Instead, he alights on the

A STRANGE WAY TO GO

Poe's death, when he was aged just forty, on 7 October 1849 was perhaps more mysterious than anything he wrote. Four days prior to his passing, he was discovered delirious on the streets of Baltimore, 'in great distress, and … in need of immediate assistance' according to one Joseph Walker, who discovered him. Poe was unable to explain how he came to be in this condition before he died, and the cause of death remains disputed. Various medical ailments have been suggested, from epilepsy to syphilis, while others have wondered whether he committed suicide or perhaps was murdered. It has even been suggested he might have been a victim of cooping – a form of electoral fraud where random voters are kidnapped and induced (for example, through enforced alcohol consumption or by beatings) to vote for a particular candidate.

culprit by recognizing the guilt contained in the emotional responses of the accused. Arguably the nearest we come to a genuine pre-Poe literary detective is Vidocq, who appeared in the *Memoirs of Eugène François Vidocq* in 1828. He was, in fact, a real person – a criminal turned police informant who rose to become head of the French national criminal investigations department and founded the world's first private detective agency. His memoirs, though, strayed regularly into the field of fiction. It has even been suggested that Vidocq himself was behind several of the crimes that he later claimed to solve.

Yet, seen as a literary creation, Vidocq displayed several of the traits of later detectives. For example, he minutely studied his crime scenes for clues and was an exponent of several cutting-edge forensic techniques, including ballistics and plaster-casting footprints. He also kept highly detailed records of crimes and liberally employed disguises. Relying on his initiative, he sifted evidence in a scientific manner, using his intellect to mine the data and unmask the wrongdoer. It was a fairly short leap of creative imagination to go from the semi-fictional Vidocq to the fully fictional Dupin.

And once Poe had opened the floodgates, there has been no stemming the tide of detective fiction, even to this day. There is, for instance, a clear lineage from Dupin to arguably the greatest literary detective of them all, Sherlock Holmes. His creator, Arthur Conan Doyle, was a self-confessed admirer of Poe, referring in his letters to 'those admirable stories of Monsieur Dupin' and describing him as 'the supreme original short story writer of all time'. Each of Poe's stories of detection, Doyle said, 'is a root from which a whole literature has developed ... Where was the detective story until Poe breathed the breath of life into it?' Holmes even gives a (admittedly barbed) nod to his great forebear in the story that introduced him to the world, *A Study in Scarlet*. 'Now, in my opinion,' Holmes tells Watson, 'Dupin was a very inferior fellow.'

In an era of rapidly increasing urbanization, Dupin and his literary descendants – whether in the hard-bitten noirs of Raymond Chandler or the Golden Age mysteries of Agatha Christie or any of the other myriad sub-genres that appeared – have allowed readers to stare into the criminal abyss from which they might shrink in real life and, in the end, to gain mastery over it. The modern world needed its detective-heroes and Dupin signposted the way.

TITLE: *ON LIBERTY*

AUTHOR: JOHN STUART MILL
DATE: 1859

. . . .

John Stuart Mill, one of the nineteenth century's great liberal thinkers, examined the relationship between the individual and authority in his masterpiece, *On Liberty*. He passionately advocated the defence of the rights of the individual under all circumstances, save when those rights impinge on the rights of another. 'That the only purpose for which power can be rightfully exercised over any member of a civilized community, against his will, is to prevent harm to others,' wrote Mill. 'His own good, either physical or moral, is not a sufficient warrant ... Over himself, over his body and mind, the individual is sovereign.' A treatise that continues to spark heated debate, its central argument has been warmly embraced by disparate audiences, from orthodox liberals to civil rights activists to libertarians.

Born in London in 1806, Mill grew up immersed in philosophy as his father, James, was himself a celebrated philosopher. Mill Jr was a precocious talent, beginning to study Greek when he was just three years old. Around the same time, his father was striking up a friendship with Jeremy Bentham, establishing an intellectual alliance based on their shared belief in, among other things, freedom of speech, religious toleration, and electoral and legal reform. John Stuart Mill thus grew up with the ideas of Bentham swirling around him (as a teenager he even lived in France for a year at the home of Bentham's brother) and it was perhaps inevitable that he would adopt Bentham's central philosophical innovation, utilitarianism – 'the greatest good for the greatest number'.

Mill began working for the East India Company when he was sixteen, remaining in its employment for some thirty years. But philosophy remained his true passion, and he was a prodigious writer, advocating personal liberty and utilitarian ideals. In 1851 he married the proto-feminist philosopher Harriet Taylor Mill, and she proved a significant influence upon his philosophical thinking.

Mill would publish a number of major works, among them *A System of Logic* (1843), *Principles of Political Economy* (1848), *Utilitarianism* (1863) and *The Subjection of Women*

(1869). But nothing was more impactful than *On Liberty*. The underpinning aim of the work was to lay out a scheme by which humanity might achieve a 'higher mode of existence'. How far, he asked, ought society to impose its power to limit the freedom of the individual? A logical reading of the doctrine of utilitarianism seemingly privileges the many over the few, but Mill made the case that it is actually by protecting the freedoms of the individual that the greatest good is achieved for society as a whole. A competent individual ought to be free to do as he wishes up to the point that they do harm to anyone else. He outlined what he considered were the three key liberties: freedom of thought and emotion (and its expression); freedom to pursue tastes, even those considered 'immoral'; and freedom to associate with other like-minded people for a common purpose. In each case the right is protected up to the point that it does harm to others.

Mill acknowledged this so-called 'harm principle' came with a good degree of complexity. Some 'harm' for example, may be accepted if it is seen to benefit the community. A new business might harm its commercial rivals by cutting into their profits or even driving them out of business, but by doing so the efficiency of the market increases to the benefit of the greater number. He also recognized that there may be unacceptable harms of omission (causing harm by not doing something, such as refusing to assist a casualty on the road) and acceptable acts of commission (an action that may cause harm, but which is excusable if all parties involved are made honestly aware of the risks – for example, paying a fireman to risk his life in the event of an inferno).

By explicitly confronting these 'exceptions', Mill sought to prove the general truth of his position.

LIVE FOREVER

On his death in 1832 aged eighty-four, Jeremy Bentham – long-time friend of Mill's father – left his body to science and it was publicly dissected. But his will included some rather stranger conditions. He made arrangements that his corpse should be turned into what he called an 'auto-icon'. This involved a process of mummification, after which his body was to be dressed and posed as he specified and put on public display in a case. His body may still be seen at University College London, although because of an unsatisfactory preserving process, it has long sported a waxwork head. The real head, meanwhile, has been the subject of a series of thefts by high-spirited students.

He considered the defence of freedom of expression to be vital to continuing progress in both the intellectual and social spheres. It was his contention that censorship denied the potential expression of truth, while it was only by allowing all opinions to be heard that one might confront and undermine those that are untruthful or hurtful. The proclivity to impose the will of the many on the few should always be resisted, he said – a tendency he observed that was strong even in supposedly free democratic societies.

In *Principles of Political Economy*, he would apply the central thesis of *On Liberty* to the world of economics. While recognizing a role for limited government intervention – for example, minting coinage, providing a narrow range of public goods and services, extracting taxation and protecting property rights – he believed, like Adam Smith before him, that the free market ought to dictate all other economic outcomes apart from in exceptional circumstances. To attempt to shackle principles of *laissez-faire*, he said, 'unless required by some great good, is a certain evil'.

In 1858, Mill lost his job as the East India Company was dismantled and in the same year he was widowed. In the years that followed, he variously served as rector of St Andrew's University and as a Member of Parliament for the Liberal Party. In such public roles, he was able to put his theories into practice and won a reputation as a radical for his support of, for example, women's rights, Irish land reform and universal education. He died in 1873, an icon of international liberalism.

His own words from *On Liberty* serve as a fitting monument to him:

> The worth of a State, in the long run, is the
> worth of the individuals composing it; and a
> State which postpones the interests of their

mental expansion and elevation, to a little more
of administrative skill, or of that semblance of it
which practice gives, in the details of business;
a State which dwarfs its men, in order that they
may be more docile instruments in its hands even
for beneficial purposes – will find that with small
men no great thing can really be accomplished;
and that the perfection of machinery to which
it has sacrificed everything, will in the end
avail it nothing, for want of the vital power
which, in order that the machine might work
more smoothly, it has preferred to banish.

TITLE: *ON THE ORIGIN OF SPECIES*

AUTHOR: CHARLES DARWIN
DATE: 1859

. . . .

Every now and again, a scientific work comes along that
not only increases humankind's collective knowledge but
also prompts a step-change in how we as a species view
ourselves and our place in the world. In the nineteenth
century, it was *On the Origin of Species by Means of Natural
Selection, or the Preservation of Favoured Races in the Struggle
for Life* (to give it its full name) – Darwin's treatise on the
subject of evolutionary biology.

Darwin compellingly argued that species evolve down through generations, changing and adapting in order to secure the greatest chance of ongoing survival. In short, those which evolve to deal with the conditions of life prevail, and those that don't, die off – a process of natural selection. It is this fundamental idea, he showed, that is responsible for the rich diversity of life that inhabits our planet. For humans, this raised some serious questions, particularly in an age of widespread faith in long-held church teachings. Specifically, much Christian theology held that humans are a species apart from the animals, designed in all their complexity by a creator-God. Darwin, though, now seemed to be saying that the story is a little more complex than that.

By the time of publication, Darwin had been honing his thesis for many years. He was building on the kernel of ideas introduced by other scientists over the previous century. In the eighteenth century, Georges Buffon was conjuring with the idea of species varieties deriving from a common ancestor. Darwin's own grandfather, Erasmus Darwin, and the naturalist Jean-Baptiste Lamarck had also discussed the transmutation of species over generations. Darwin was also influenced by Thomas Malthus's theories on human population growth, which chimed with his ideas on the competitive nature of survival.

Darwin had initially studied medicine but soon found his true passion was the natural sciences. In the 1830s, he spent almost five years travelling around the world aboard HMS *Beagle*, during which time he gathered the notes and data that were to underpin *On the Origin of Species*. In 1839,

Darwin's journal from these travels was published (becoming popularly known as *The Voyage of the Beagle*), and making Darwin something of a celebrity in Victorian society.

CHALLENGING ORTHODOXY

The fundamental social and religious implications of Darwin's work were famously explored in the so-called Scopes Monkey Trial, conducted in Dayton, Tennessee, in 1925. On trial was high school teacher, John Scopes, accused of violating state law by teaching human evolution. He was initially convicted but the verdict was later overturned on a technicality. Scopes, though, had implicated himself in order to bring attention to the tension that existed between those in the Presbyterian Church who believed that religious teaching should respond to the expansion of scientific knowledge and those who believed that the words of the Bible should always take precedence.

The voyage had left him suspecting that species were not fixed, but rather subject to adaptation. But finding himself a man in high demand, it was only in 1842 that he wrote a first brief abstract of his developing theory

– notes that comprised some thirty-five pages. Over the next couple of years, he expanded this into an essay over two hundred pages in length. Around the same time, a book by Robert Chambers popularized the idea of species transmutation. Although it was altogether a much less wide-ranging theory than Darwin would eventually launch onto the world, it eased the path for what was to come.

Meanwhile, Darwin was intent on gathering more data. For example, over a period of several years he studied barnacles to detect indicators of their evolution, becoming a world authority on the species. In a similar vein, he turned himself into an expert pigeon breeder. By the mid-1850s, he was fully dedicated to progressing his theory of natural selection as a driver of evolutionary divergence. But there was now another player on the field – naturalist Alfred Russel Wallace was developing his own thesis on the subject.

The two men corresponded and, by 1858, it was apparent that they were heading in similar, if not identical, directions. Spooked that he might be beaten to the punch and that his years of work would be for nothing, Darwin agreed to co-publish and present a collection of papers with Wallace in London. Few outside the specialized scientific community took much notice, though. Darwin now devoted himself to completing *On the Origin of Species*, which appeared the following year with this startling summation of natural selection:

> As many more individuals of each species are born than can possibly survive; and as, consequently, there is a frequently recurring struggle for existence, it follows that any being, if it vary however slightly in any manner profitable to itself, under the complex and sometimes varying conditions of life, will have a better chance of surviving, and thus be naturally selected. From the strong principle of inheritance, any selected variety will tend to propagate its new and modified form.

This was truly revolutionary stuff. Not least, if nature evolves to survive and flourish, where does that leave the idea of a godhead pulling the strings? For the time being, Darwin was careful not to overreach himself. He did not extend his theory to the human species, although he did give a tantalizing glimpse of what it all might mean for us with a line in the last chapter: 'Light will be thrown on the origin of Man and his history.' He also noted: 'There is grandeur in this view of life, with its several powers, having been originally breathed into a few forms or into one; and that, whilst this planet has gone cycling on according to the fixed law of gravity, from so simple a beginning endless forms most beautiful and most wonderful have been, and are being, evolved.' From the second edition of the book, he added the words 'by the Creator' after 'breathed'.

Fearful of 'only add[ing] to the prejudices against my views', it was not until 1871 that Darwin publicly tackled human evolution in *The Descent of Man, and Selection in Relation to Sex*. By then, the theory of Darwinian evolution had widespread acceptance. Of course, not everyone was convinced. John Herschel, a scientist venerated by Darwin, dismissed the theory as the 'law of higgledy-piggledy'. Others, more damagingly, abused Darwin's work for their own ends – in particular, advocates of 'social Darwinism' who espoused ideas of 'survival of the fittest' to justify theories of racial superiority and eugenics. But away from the hands of the cranks, Darwin's theory of evolution has proved extraordinarily durable, underpinning over a century and a half of natural science and spilling into other areas as diverse as agriculture, medicine and computer science.

TITLE: *INCIDENTS IN THE LIFE OF A SLAVE GIRL*

AUTHOR: HARRIET JACOBS
DATE: 1861

. . . .

Incidents in the Life of a Slave Girl, a pseudonymous autobiography of a fugitive slave, caused a minor sensation when it was published in 1861. Jacobs renamed herself as Linda Brent in the book, which tells the story of her time in slavery and her fight for freedom for herself and her children. Jacobs intended the work to convey the particular horrors of slavery from a female perspective in the hope that it would draw more white women towards the abolitionist movement. For a long time, the work was all but forgotten, but it has come to be regarded as a classic not only of the abolitionist movement but of feminist literature too.

Jacobs was born into slavery in 1813 in Edenton, North Carolina. In her early years she was taught to read and write by her female owner, an education very few of her fellow slaves ever enjoyed. But her life took a turn for the worse when she was twelve years old and her mistress's death saw ownership transferred to a man who sexually abused her – a crime compounded by the fact that his interest in her inspired the ire of his wife.

As a teen, Jacobs fell in love with a free black man but her owner prevented the relationship developing. She then became involved with a white lawyer, whose two children she would bear while still in her teens. Her son and daughter inherited her slave status and their master continued his cruel treatment, sending them to a relative's plantation and vowing to see that they (along with Jacobs' brother, John) were sold to another slave-owner out of state to ensure their permanent separation from her.

In 1835, Jacobs made the decision to escape her servitude, an enterprise that involved hiding in a swamp and then spending some seven years in what was described as a 'garret' – a tiny crawl space above her grandmother's home. Here she spent much time reading, not least the Bible but newspapers as well. In the meantime, her brother managed to escape from his master (ultimately finding his way to Boston), while her children's lawyer-father intervened to ensure that they were not sold out of state, although he failed to win them their freedom.

After seven years in the crawl space, Jacobs embarked on the next stage of her life, fleeing to New York via Philadelphia. In New York, she was taken on as a nanny by Mary Stace Willis, wife of the author Nathaniel Parker Willis (who was the best-renumerated magazine writer of his day). But still her former owner pursued her. In order to escape him, she had stints with her brother in Boston, then a hotbed of the abolitionist movement, and also in England when she once more worked for the Willis family.

In 1852, again under threat of being reclaimed by her former slave-owners, Jacobs became a free woman when the second wife of the widowed Nathaniel Parker Willis bought her liberty. By this time, her brother John was working for the abolitionist movement headed by William Lloyd Garrison in

New York and staying with two of its most prominent figures, Amy and Isaac Post. It was John and Amy who began to persuade Jacobs to write her life story.

UNCLE TOM'S CABIN

Several years before Jacobs struggled to find a publisher, Harriet Beecher Stowe had enormous commercial success with her novel, *Uncle Tom's Cabin*. It is thought to have been the bestselling novel of the nineteenth century. A white abolitionist, Stowe based the book on a number of first-hand accounts, and it has been credited with fundamentally changing white American attitudes to slavery as the US careered towards civil war. But it has also come to be seen as one that damagingly reinforced assorted white prejudices about people of colour through its reliance upon racial stereotypes. Today, 'Uncle Tom' operates as an insult addressed to those who might be considered to betray their own cultural heritage by their servility to others.

Having immersed herself in the ideas of anti-slavery, Jacobs reflected: 'The more my mind had become enlightened, the more difficult it was for me to consider myself an article of property.' She composed *Incidents in the Life of a Slave Girl* between 1853 and 1858, while working once more as a nanny for the Willis family. It took her a further two years to find a publisher and the book finally reached market in 1861.

Hers was by no means the first book written by a slave. The autobiographical *Narrative of the Life of Frederick Douglass* had been an enormous success back in the 1840s. But Jacobs' experiences as a woman in slavery added another dimension to her work. Nor did she shy away from depicting the brutality of her treatment, including her sexual abuse, or from how her refusal to conform to the expectations of entitled white patriarchy contributed to many of the worst experiences of her life. She also took on such potentially divisive subjects as religion and the Church. In particular, she highlighted the deep Christian faith of many slaves (her own grandmother suggested they should accept their slavery as an expression of God's will) and contrasted it with the hypocritical conduct of so-called God-fearing slave-owners.

The book received positive notices from the outset and secured a significant readership through its promotion via the abolitionist networks operating across the United States. On its publication in Britain, a reviewer for the *London Daily News* described Jacobs' character in the book as a 'heroine' who exemplified 'endurance and persistency in the struggle for liberty'. Few who read the book could reasonably conclude that slavery was anything but a terrible thing. Along with Frederick Douglass's work, the abolitionists had a pair of extremely powerful first-hand accounts to support their cause.

Yet *Incidents in the Life of a Slave Girl* soon became a forgotten work. Moreover, Jacobs' literacy and her ability to write a narrative full of melodramatic verve (reflecting the commercial tastes of the day) brought her critics. Some simply refused to believe this was autobiographical. Often, it was suggested that Jacobs was not even the true author. Only in relatively recent years have academic researchers uncovered the various source materials that substantiate her story. It is perhaps telling as to the strength of her communication skills and the horror of what she endured that she became the subject of such interrogations. Surely this cannot be true, her critics secretly hoped. But, to our collective shame, it was.

The work enjoyed a renaissance in the 1960s after many years in the literary wilderness, driven by the combined emergence of the feminist and civil rights movements. And while legalized slavery may have been consigned to the past, her voice continues to ring out, advocating for justice for the oppressed. As she said of her motivation for writing the book: 'Reader, it is not to awaken sympathy for myself that I am telling you truthfully what I suffered. I do it to kindle a flame of compassion in your hearts for my sisters who are still in bondage.'

TITLE: *DAS KAPITAL*

AUTHOR: KARL MARX
DATE: 1867–83

. . . .

Das Kapital (*Capital*) is the *magnum opus* of Karl Marx, his 'Critique of Political Economy' that, although much of it was published after his death, fuelled (along with his much shorter 1848 work, co-written with Friedrich Engels, *The Communist Manifesto*) the socialist revolutions that defined a large part of twentieth-century history. The work's central theme is that capitalism only thrives through the exploitation of labour, and Marx aims to trace its historical circumstance and explore the mechanisms by which it functions.

Marx was born in Prussia in 1818 and read law and philosophy at a number of German universities, before moving to Paris with his wife in the 1840s and then, after expulsion from France, on to London. Espousing radical, socialist views, he was also profoundly influenced by Hegel, believing existence not to be a fixed reality but rather a process of historical change. In terms of humanity, Marx identified four major stages of human history that he described in socio-economic terms. First, an ancient system of common ownership, superseded by one of private property and slavery, which in turn fell to a system of feudalism, itself replaced by capitalism. Every stage, he suggested, had a common denominator in that one social group dominated until another dislodged it in a violent transition. He predicted that capitalism would itself be overcome by communism in just such a way. As he put it in the *Manifesto*: 'The history of all hitherto existing society is the history of class struggles.'

If the *Communist Manifesto* set out Marx's vision of the future and was a call to arms, *Das Kapital* was his attempt to give it intellectual weight and gravitas through an in-depth – and sometimes unwieldy – combination of historical, economic and sociological analysis. He goes into such technical areas as the nature of commodities, capital accumulation, the business cycle, wage labour (i.e. the relationship between workers and employers) and the theory of surplus value (i.e. the value created by a worker above the level of the wages they receive).

According to Marx, it all went to prove that capitalism inevitably exploits the labour force, which in turn renders the whole system unstable. Workers (the *proletariat*) remain poor because they can never access the profits of their own work. Moreover, because the nature of that work tends to be repetitive, they become little more than automatons with diminishing quality of life. Yet, by facilitating the cycle of surplus value, the workers perpetuate the very system that enchains them.

The means of production, meanwhile, are concentrated in the hands of the property-owning class (the *bourgeoisie*), a number in diminishing proportion to the ever-swelling ranks of the proletariat. They are permitted, indeed enabled, to reap the profits of others' labour by an establishment that, according to Marx, is rooted in a history of conquest and plunder. As the bourgeoisie enjoy the benefits of improved technology, increasing their profits while requiring fewer workers, the number of unemployed, disenchanted members of the proletariat increases until the overthrow of the bourgeoisie and the collapse of capitalism becomes an inevitability. Another stage in the cycle of socio-economic change that defines human existence.

WHERE ENGELS DARED TO TREAD

Friedrich Engels, born in Prussia in 1821, is often regarded as something like the junior partner in his relationship with Marx. We speak, after all, of Marxism, not Engelsism. A journalist and son of a wealthy mill-owner, he was nonetheless a significant figure in his own right, and one who facilitated much of Marx's work on *Das Kapital*. Marx rarely had money to spare and lived a life of near destitution back in London after the failed revolutions of 1848. Were it not for the handouts of Engels, his fate would have been highly uncertain and it seems unlikely that *Das Kapital* would ever have seen the light of day.

Marx had high hopes of witnessing first-hand some of the social change he predicted. When Europe was in the grip of several revolutions in 1848 – in France, Prussia, Italy and the Austro-Hungarian Empire – the moment seemed to have arrived but those revolutions were soon snuffed out one by one. Marx, who had gone to the continent to see events for himself, was profoundly disappointed by what historian G. M. Trevelyan has called a 'turning point in modern history that modern history failed to turn'.

Marx returned to London, doubling down in *Das Kapital* on the ideas he introduced in the *Communist Manifesto*. The first of three bulky volumes appeared in 1867, but the second and third volumes would not appear until after his death in 1883. His old friend Engels edited them into publishable shape from the notes Marx left behind. Still, it would be many decades before Marx's famous summons, 'Workers of the World, Unite!', came to pass. In 1917 Russia established the world's first communist state, following the Bolshevik-led overthrow of the bourgeoisie just as Marx predicted. Many more nations followed over the course of the century, across the continents and including the world's most populous country, China. None, however, ushered in the nirvana that Marx had dreamed of, instead serving up a *mélange* of popular dissatisfaction, poverty, leader cults and tyranny.

Today, 'Marxist' is often used as a slur by those on the political right against anybody deemed in opposition to their beliefs: a catch-all term to signify a failed political philosophy. Yet, for all that Marxism in the twentieth century failed to deliver on its promise of social and economic justice for the masses, its figurehead produced a body of work that altered the world in fundamental ways. Moreover, if Marxism is not the answer, it remains highly unclear – in a world of increasing inequality and subject to devastating cycles of boom and bust – that unfettered capitalism is either. Marx might not have found the solution, but he may have identified a problem.

TITLE: *WAR AND PEACE*

AUTHOR: LEO TOLSTOY
DATE: 1869

. . . .

War and Peace, regarded as among the finest novels of world literature, tells the story of several aristocratic families as they adapt to their life in Russia in the years leading up to and after the Napoleonic invasion of 1812. Tolstoy said of his book that it is 'not a novel, even less is it a poem, and still less a historical chronicle'. Written in the realist style, it does, however, contain elements of all three. Epic in scale and wrapped in existential angst, it is a study of a world in flux. Through his expansive cast of characters, Tolstoy examines how individuals respond under the pressures of war, political and social upheaval, and spiritual uncertainty. A century and a half after its publication, it stands as a monumental literary achievement that continues to speak of the human condition and how we may rise and fall in the face of an uncertain world. 'Seize the moments of happiness,' he writes at one point, 'love and be loved! That is the only reality in the world, all else is folly.'

Tolstoy was born in 1828, just a few years after the events that he narrates. Born into an aristocratic family, he was a rather dissolute youth. In 1851, faced with significant gambling debts, he joined the army and saw action in the Crimean War and was present at the almost year-long siege of Sevastopol. Although recognized for his military service, these experiences deeply traumatized him. Leaving the army and embarking on extensive travels around Europe, he became increasingly radical in his views, which were rooted in his fundamentalist Christian beliefs. He came to question the legitimacy of government, espousing various anarchist points of view and was a noted pacifist and advocate of non-violence.

No less a figure than Gandhi would say of him that his 'life has been devoted to replacing the method of violence for removing tyranny or securing reform by the method of non-resistance to evil. He would meet hatred expressed in violence by love expressed in selfsuffering.' Although he was yet to fully explore some of these views at the time of writing *War and Peace*, he was nonetheless much removed from the fast-living young aristocrat from before his army days.

ANNA KARENINA

In opposition to the world at large, Tolstoy considered his true first novel to be not *War and Peace* but *Anna Karenina*, another multifaceted epic set against the backdrop of nineteenth-century imperial Russian high society. Similarly acclaimed as a high watermark of global literature, it repeated the trick of taking a psychologically engaging drama and infusing it with a sense of universal truth. As the English poet and critic Matthew Arnold commented, 'We are not to take *Anna Karenina* as a work of art, we are to take it as a piece of life.'

The novel begins in St Petersburg in 1805, at a time when Napoleon's domination of Western Europe was starting to ring alarm bells in the East. The book is in some senses the story of a clash of cultures, of two great civilizations under the sway of contrasting leaders: Napoleon and Tsar Alexander. Fittingly, the action starts at the party of a society hostess, the very epitome of ordered, civilized society.

But it is not long before it becomes apparent that the book's many characters are little more than flotsam and jetsam cast about by the tides of history. In Tolstoy's own words: 'Every action of theirs [great men], that seems to them an act of their own free will, is in an historical sense not free at all, but in bondage to the whole course of previous history, and predestined from all eternity.'

The novel explores the stories of nearly six hundred characters from all walks of life – from civilians to servicemen, peasants to nobility. But it is for its high-born characters that it is best known. The likes of the central protagonist Pierre Bezukhov, the wealthy but socially awkward illegitimate son of a count (a figure whom Tolstoy based partly on himself), Prince Andrei Bolkonsky, his best friend who leaves his family to fight against Napoleon, and Natasha Rostov, the kindly and beautiful daughter of a noble family who grows close to both Pierre and Andrei.

For its Russian readership, the novel has become absorbed into the national psyche. The story of Russia's ultimate defeat of the invader from the West, culminating in the wretched Battle of Borodino depicted so evocatively by Tolstoy, informs Russia's sense of its self even now. During the Second World War the book was distributed to Soviet troops, many of whom were reported to be more moved by its descriptions of war than by the battle scenes they were witnessing first-hand. To understand the background to perpetual East–West tensions, *War and Peace* is not a bad place to start.

But the book quickly won admirers far from Russia's borders, based on its universality. Comprising 361 chapters, it depicts life in all its glory, from ballrooms to battlefields. It would be difficult to read it and not feel connection with at least some of what goes on. As Henry James once said of Tolstoy, he was a 'monster harnessed to his great subject – all of life'.

'History is the life of nations and of humanity,' Tolstoy wrote. 'To seize and put into words, to describe directly the life of humanity or even of a single nation, appears impossible.' And yet somehow he succeeded. As evidence of the book's reach across time, it is worth noting that Nelson Mandela identified it as his favourite novel during his long years in prison.

Tolstoy's fellow Russian, the writer Isaak Babel (1894–1940), encapsulated Tolstoy's ability to transcend from the specific to the universal, to take the chaos of Napoleonic Russia and frame it to speak of the human soul. 'If the world could write by itself,' Babel said, 'it would write like Tolstoy.'

TITLE: *THE INTERPRETATION OF DREAMS*

AUTHOR: SIGMUND FREUD
DATE: 1899
....

'The interpretation of dreams is the royal road to a knowledge of the unconscious activities of the mind.' So wrote Sigmund Freud, the father of psychoanalysis, in what became his most famous work, *The Interpretation of*

Dreams. Published at the dawn of a new century, Freud hoped it would spur a Copernican revolution in the study of the mind. Instead, it took years to sell more than a few hundred copies. But gradually, Freud's revolutionary ideas seeped into the mainstream and became a staple of popular culture. Moreover, he provided us with a lexicon of terms that remain in widespread use today. If nothing else, Freud made it acceptable as never before for people to try to make sense of themselves – and we have never really looked back.

Born in Freiburg in the Austrian Empire in 1856, Freud had a quite unremarkable early career. Having qualified as a doctor of medicine from the University of Vienna, he was a specialist in neurology with a passion for psychology, leading him to study abnormalities of the mind like hysteria and neuroses. However, his engagement with dreams saw him extend his practice to exploration of the mind as a whole – both 'abnormal' and 'normal'. In doing so he birthed psychoanalysis, which he would describe in 1925 as 'the starting point of a new, a deeper science of the mind which would be ... indispensable for the understanding of the normal'.

In *The Interpretation of Dreams*, he laid out a model of the mind divided into three distinct areas – the Conscious, the Preconscious and the Subconscious:

- Conscious – that part of the mind taken to comprise those things of which we are aware, and that we may contemplate and discourse upon in a rational manner

- Preconscious – made up of all those ideas and memories that are latent most of the time but that may easily become conscious. (For instance, a mobile phone number, which may not immediately roll off the tongue but which can be dredged up as required without too much effort)

- Subconscious – those desires, impulses and wishes that are normally inaccessible to the conscious mind but that can significantly influence our behaviour

Just as only a small proportion of an iceberg is ever visible above the water line, so in Freud's model only the Conscious can be 'seen' (or at least, recognized), while the vast majority of the mind (i.e. the Preconscious and Subconscious) goes 'unseen' beneath the waterline. Yet, so Freud argued, dreams allow us to examine what is going on under the waterline. As he put it: 'Dreams are never concerned with trivialities; we do not allow our sleep to be disturbed by trifles.' He believed dreams allow us to safely address those thoughts and feelings that are too shameful or unsettling to confront in our conscious existence.

A FISHY TALE

On one notable occasion, one of Freud's patients related a dream in which she held a wriggling fish in her hand. Doubtless a keen student of her doctor's work, she confidently announced to him that the fish surely represented a penis. Freud had a different view, though. He knew the woman's mother disapproved of her appointments with him and that she was also an avid astrologer born under the sign of Pisces. The fish, Freud held, was far more likely to represent the patient's mother than a penis – a mix-up that neatly emphasized the subjective nature of dream interpretation.

He claimed that dreams communicate information in two distinct ways. First, there is manifest content, the events of the dream as recalled by the dreamer. But there is also latent content, the unconscious ideas that lie hidden and coded behind the manifest content. Manifest content, he contended, results from sensory experiences while asleep, combined with recent worries and concerns ('day residue'). But the really interesting stuff is in the latent content, which comprises repressed wishes from the subconscious that attach themselves to the manifest content in a disguised manner (a process known as 'dreamwork').

The two chief modes of disguising unconscious thought that Freud identified were condensation (where multiple ideas, objects and themes are brought together in a single object or person) and displacement (in which meaning is transferred to a different person, object or action). For instance, if you see a man being stabbed in front of a blue car, you may displace your fear of the assailant into a fear of blue cars. 'Dream-displacement and dream-condensation,' Freud said, 'are the two governing factors to whose activity we may in essence ascribe the form assumed by dreams.'

He made other bold assertions too, perhaps most famously: 'When the work of interpretation has been completed, we perceive that a dream is the fulfilment of a wish.' Expanding on the subject, he said: 'The more one is occupied with the solution of dreams, the readier one becomes to acknowledge that the majority of the dreams of adults deal with sexual material and give expression to erotic wishes.' Such claims inevitably caused a good deal of outrage in turn-of-the-century European society, where the notion that one's deepest passions and feelings might be read in one's dreams caused much discomfort. Perhaps wary of this, Freud was somewhat cautious on the subject. 'In dream-interpretation,' he said, 'this importance of the sexual complexes must never be forgotten, though one must not, of course, exaggerate it to the exclusion of all other factors.'

One of Freud's pivotal suggestions also left him open to potential mockery – his claim that it is possible to interpret the 'hidden' meaning of all sorts of signs and symbols evident in even the most innocuous details of a dream. Take, for example, his observation: 'It is perfectly true that dreams contain symbolizations of bodily organs and functions, that water in a dream often points to a urinary stimulus, and that the male genitals can be represented by an upright stick or a pillar, and so on.' Given the inevitably subjective nature of such interpretation, it has been apocryphally suggested that even Freud was once moved to note that 'Sometimes a cigar is just a cigar.'

There is no doubt that *The Interpretation of Dreams* is deeply flawed as a scientific treatise. Much of what Freud had a tendency to frame as scientific truth has been shown up as speculation, opinion or conjecture in the decades since his death in 1939. From his structural models of the psyche, his theories of psychosexual development and his methodology of dream interpretation, little has survived intact. Yet still his book helped to bring a profound energy to the scientific study of the psyche that remains to this day.

Freud was, for example, responsible for a sea-change in attitudes to mental illness. Where people had once been cast out as variously physiologically compromised, morally degenerate or even agents of devilry, Freud offered hope that the causes of psychological imbalance could be discovered and addressed. More fundamentally, he originated concepts that allow us to view the world differently. He redirected our gaze from the world around us and its constructions – the universe, society, theology – to the world within us – our psyches. It is worth noting that the window above Freud's desk was adorned with a mirror that permanently enabled him to look at himself even while he stared out on the world.

Without *The Interpretation of Dreams* and Freud's other works, our daily discourse would be devoid of such terms as the unconscious, the ego and the id, the libido, the Oedipus Complex, penis envy, the Freudian slip, the psychiatrist's couch, anally retentive … Indeed, he is one of those few individuals whose name has even gained adjectival status. As the psychologist and Freud academic John Kihlstrom once noted: 'More than Einstein or Watson and Crick, more than Hitler or Lenin, Roosevelt or Kennedy, more than Picasso, Eliot, or Stravinsky, more than the Beatles or Bob Dylan, Freud's influence on modern culture has been profound and long-lasting.'

V

1900 ONWARDS

TITLE: *GENERAL THEORY OF RELATIVITY*

AUTHOR: ALBERT EINSTEIN
DATE: 1916

. . . .

Indisputably the most famous scientific paper of the twentieth century, Albert Einstein's *General Theory of Relativity* ushered in a new scientific age, with implications for the world both good and bad. It demanded a reappraisal of our fundamental understanding of the nature of time and space and showed us that gravity does not function quite as Isaac Newton had envisaged. It also prompted a complete rethink of how we viewed the universe, from the sub-atomic level up. Among the many outcomes of his work, he laid the groundwork for modern quantum mechanics (although he questioned the concept for the duration of his life) and ushered in the nuclear age, a legacy with which he subsequently always struggled.

For a long while, it seemed unlikely that Einstein would make much of a mark on the world, let alone become perhaps the most famous scientist who has ever lived (and definitely the most recognizable). Born in 1879, he was a late developer when it came to speaking and was nicknamed 'the dopey one' by his own father. Although it was soon clear he was gifted in the areas of maths and physics, his academic career stuttered. After graduating from the Swiss Federal Polytechnic School in Zürich, he struggled to find an academic posting. Instead, he took a day job at the Swiss

Patent Office, exploring his passion for theoretical physics in his own time.

Then, in 1905, over the course of a series of revolutionary papers, he announced himself to the world – a full decade before publication of the *General Theory*. The first paper, which he described as 'very revolutionary', dealt with radiation and the energy properties of light, and would prove crucial to the development of quantum theory. The second was on the 'determination of the true size of atoms' and the third was an investigation of Brownian motion using statistical analysis that confirmed the actual existence of atoms and molecules. The fourth, meanwhile, was the *Special Theory of Relativity*, which examined the electrodynamics of moving bodies and, according to Einstein in a letter to a friend at the time, 'employs a modification of the theory of space and time'. It is difficult to think of a more understated way to announce that you are about to fundamentally change humankind's understanding of the universe.

Einstein established that the laws of physics are the same for all observers moving at constant velocity relative to each other, and that the speed of light in a vacuum is constant. He envisaged a cosmos in which the familiar three dimensions of space meld with time to form 'spacetime', where single events may appear to occur at different times to different observers. In layman's terms, where Newton had seemingly shown that space and time were absolute, Einstein showed that they were not. This was every bit as earth-shattering as anything Copernicus or Darwin had thrown at an unready world. Here was a scientist saying that not even the way your clock ticked or the space it inhabited on your mantelpiece were quite as they seemed. But where others saw uncertainty, he saw unchangeability in the nature of fundamental physical laws. Indeed, he had originally planned to call the paper the *Theory of Invariance*.

The *Special Theory* led on to one final paper that year, just three pages long. Its conclusions, though, were startling. Einstein had found that a body's mass is a proportional measure of its energy content. In other words, mass and energy are different presentations of the same thing. An insight that would come to be illustrated with the most famous equation in history: $E=mc^2$ (energy = mass × the speed of light squared). This discovery – that something very small could contain an awful lot of energy – was the stepping stone to the nuclear age.

Even as the rest of the world was trying to come to terms with the revelations contained within the *Special Theory*, Einstein was obsessing over its shortfalls. Specifically, he was unhappy that it applied only under circumstances of motion at constant velocity. Furthermore, Newton's universe relied on the notion that gravity is an instantaneous force but Einstein realized this could not be right since he had established that nothing (including a physical interaction such as gravity) could travel faster than the speed of light.

Many of his greatest intellectual breakthroughs came as a result of complex thought experiments, which he conducted in search of 'great leaps forward of the imagination'. On this occasion, he focused on the sensations experienced by a person free-falling while contained in an enclosed space such as an elevator. The subject, he came to realize, would have no idea whether they were in the grip of a gravitational field or in gravity-free deep space. It would take Einstein a further gruelling eight years, but from this thought experiment would grow the *General Theory*.

THE NOBEL PRIZE

Einstein was awarded a Nobel Prize for his work but not, as you might expect, for his work on relativity. In 1921, the awarding committee was unable to reach agreement as to whether his theory qualified for the Prize, as under Nobel rules it needed to be classed as a 'discovery or invention'. There was a vocal body that argued it was not a 'law' that had been 'discovered', but a 'theory' that had been 'proposed'. So, a compromise was reached and he was instead given the Prize for the first of his 1905 papers on the law of the photoelectric effect, rather than for the theory that was famous the world over.

One of the chief problems he faced was that his theory required new types of mathematics, including a form of geometry that went beyond that which Euclid had defined. In the end, an old student friend, Marcel Grossmann, came to the rescue, navigating him through the non-Euclidean mathematics of Bernhard Riemann (1826–66) and the calculus of Gregorio Ricci-Curbastro (1853–1925).

By the end of 1915, Einstein was confident that he had suitably refined his theory and had the maths to back it up. Over a series of four lectures that year he laid out what he considered to be 'the most valuable discovery of my life'. Where Newton described a universe in which an apple falls to the ground from a tree because gravity exerts a force of attraction, Einstein redefined gravity as a curvature of space-time.

Four years later, the first observable evidence for his postulations was recorded and overnight he went from being a moderately renowned figure of modern science to a global superstar whose name resonated in even the least scientific households. As he himself explained it: 'The practical man need not worry … From the philosophical aspect, however, it has importance, as it alters the conceptions of time and space which are necessary to philosophical speculations and conceptions.'

Einstein carried on his theoretical explorations even as he became an international public figure. Alongside the science, he became a notable campaigner against authoritarianism and also against the atom bomb that he unintentionally helped to create. Today, the impact of the *General Theory* is around us, everywhere. It is there in how we have come to perceive ourselves within the universe. It is in the mysteries of the black holes that his science predicted. But it is also there in the everyday, in our televisions and the GPS systems that steer our cars. In fellow physicist Max

Born's estimation, the *General Theory* was nothing less than 'the greatest feat of human thinking about nature – the most amazing combination of philosophical penetration, physical intuition and mathematical skill'.

TITLE: *THE DIARY OF A YOUNG GIRL*

AUTHOR: ANNE FRANK
DATE: 1947

. . . .

The Diary of a Young Girl (also commonly known as *The Diary of Anne Frank*) is the true-life diary of Anne Frank, the teenage daughter of a German family living in Amsterdam during the Second World War. Written in an affecting tone, it tells the story of Anne and her family as they spend some two years evading capture by the occupying Nazi forces, living in an annex attached to the premises of her father's business. That we know the tragic fate awaiting Anne and her loved ones gives the diary an emotive power arguably unsurpassed in twentieth-century literature.

Anne was just four years old when her parents decided to move the family from Frankfurt to Amsterdam as Hitler tightened his grip on Germany. As Jews, the Franks were acutely aware of the rising tide of anti-Semitic persecution and hoped to find safety in the Netherlands. Anne's father, Otto, established a successful business, trading in pectin, a gelling agent used in food manufacturing. However, the family's hopes of outrunning Hitler's grasp faded as the Netherlands was overrun in 1940.

THE DUTY TO REFLECT

Anne Frank's diary counts as arguably the most famous of a vast swathe of writing related to the Holocaust. Every year, new first-person accounts of that horror are discovered and published. In 1986, Elie Wiesel received the Nobel Prize for Literature, having risen to fame with publication of his memoir, *Night*, in 1960. The Nobel Committee described him as 'a messenger to mankind; his message is one of peace, atonement, and human dignity'. Primo Levi, an Italian-born Auschwitz survivor, published his own world-renowned recollections, *If This Is a Man*, in 1947 and later warned that the events of the 1940s might be repeated. 'For this reason,' he said, 'it is everyone's duty to reflect on what happened.'

By the summer of 1942, Jews were suffering deportations to concentration camps. In July that year, Anne's older sister, Margot, was summoned for 'labour duty' in Germany. It was the warning shot that spurred Anne's parents into action. The family immediately went into hiding in the annex of Otto's business, its door hidden by a bookcase. They were supported in living there by a small band of confidantes, who supplied them with food and other essentials. For the duration of their exile in the secret apartment, the Franks were able to keep their presence secret from all but these few people despite the premises being populated by employees throughout the working week. Anne would in due course note that while others showed their heroism in battle, the family's helpers proved theirs each day by their affection and good spirits.

Anne received her diary (or, rather a checked red autograph book that she used as her diary) on her thirteenth birthday, 12 June 1942. The entries start on that day, with Anne keen to confide everything to it. She wrote that, in lieu of a companion to whom she could reveal everything, the book would become a source of support and comfort.

Over the months and years, it evolved into a record not only of Anne's existence in the annex but also of her inner life. She talked about further arrivals sharing the space to escape the Nazis – the Van Pels, consisting of Hermann (her father's business partner), Auguste (his wife), Peter (their son), and later a dentist called Fritz Pfeffer.

Anne found the appearance of these newcomers a trial at first, not least because she had to share her room with Peter, who was of a similar age to herself. Her diary entries tell us much about her relationships – her closeness to her father, the comparative distance with her mother and her great affection for her sister. She covers an enormous range of subjects but what most distinctly emerges is Anne as an ordinary girl facing the challenges of transitioning from childhood to the teenage years in the most extraordinary of circumstances. Among the many subplots is her evolving relationship with Peter, with whom she grows very close before they gradually drift apart again.

On Christmas Eve of 1943, she confided how being shut up for a year and a half was taking its toll. She talked of her wish to ride a bike, to dance, to look at the world and 'to feel young and know that I'm free'. But, she realizes, there is nothing to be gained by feeling sorry for herself. 'Where would that get us?' she asked plaintively.

In March 1944, Anne's diary entries already amounted to a significant body of work when she heard an announcement on the wireless by a member of the exiled Dutch government in London. The minister announced plans eventually to gather together diaries and other personal records of the

German occupation once the war was over. Anne took it upon herself to rewrite and edit her existing diary with this in mind, creating what are now known as a 'Version A' and 'Version B'. The idea of the diary serving a wider purpose appealed, as she harboured a dream to become a famous writer and journalist. By this stage, all diary entries are addressed to 'Kitty', the diary now fully personified as confidante.

The final entry in the diary is dated 1 August 1944. Just three days later, their hiding-place was discovered and its inhabitants arrested. It has long been assumed that the location of the eight was betrayed to the authorities, although others have more recently suggested their discovery may have been the result of misfortune instead, with the police raid originally focused on alleged ration fraud. Regardless, the result was much the same. They were deported to various concentration camps. These included Auschwitz, but Anne was later moved to Bergen-Belsen, enduring myriad horrors along the way. She died, aged just fifteen, in February or March 1945, probably during a typhus outbreak. The camp was liberated by Allied troops just a few weeks later. Only her father, Otto, would survive the war.

When he returned to Amsterdam, he was given his daughter's diaries by someone who had rescued them immediately after the raid on the annex. At first, he struggled to find a publisher. It was thought there would be little appetite to revisit the horrors of the war and the crimes against Jews so soon after the events.

Otto then passed on the diaries to historian Jan Romein, who quickly recognized their value. 'This apparently inconsequential diary by a child,' he wrote in a newspaper article in 1946, 'this "de profundis" stammered out in a child's voice, embodies all the hideousness of fascism, more so than all the evidence of Nuremberg [the Nazi War Trials] put together.' The following year, *The Annex: Diary Notes 14 June 1942–1 August 1944* was published in Europe and caused a sensation. Five years later, it was published in the US as *Anne Frank: The Diary of a Young Girl*, complete with an introduction by First Lady Eleanor Roosevelt. It has gone on to sell tens of millions of copies, becoming a staple on school curriculums and inspiring plays, films and television shows.

It remains perhaps the best-known first-hand record of the Jewish experience in the Second World War, and as such stands as a historical document of immense importance. But it is ultimately an intensely moving record of what it is to be human. And amid the tragedy, Anne emerges as an emblem of hope. Not least in her assertion: 'I still believe, in spite of everything, that people are truly good at heart.'

TITLE: *NINETEEN EIGHTY-FOUR*

AUTHOR: GEORGE ORWELL
DATE: 1949

. . . .

Written in a century scarred by the excesses of totalitarian regimes espousing ideologies across the political spectrum,

Nineteen Eighty-Four is a dystopian masterpiece warning of the consequences of one-party authoritarianism. It has seeped into international culture, not least because of an array of memorable phrases and ideas that set the terms of discussion about such regimes. For those who had come to consider it a novel of the past, it has also found a disconcerting new relevance in the tumultuous international political landscape of the twenty-first century.

Written in the 1940s, the '1984' depicted in the novel is one of great bleakness. Control of the world has been divided into three totalitarian superstates that are in a state of perpetual conflict. The action takes place in one of these states, Oceania (the others being Eurasia and Eastasia), and specifically in the region formerly known as Great Britain but now renamed Airstrip One. Rule is in the hands of 'The Party', which operates under the Ingsoc ideology (an abbreviation for English Socialism). Its enigmatic figurehead is Big Brother, around whom an all-encompassing cult of personality is constructed. The regime ensures conformity by the imposition of mass surveillance and the brutal repression of all dissent. Those who fall foul of the Party become 'unpersons' and are disappeared, all record that they ever existed destroyed.

The central protagonist is Winston Smith, who works at the Ministry of Truth (essentially, a ministry of propaganda), where he is involved in the editing of historical records in order to keep them in line with current government narratives. He is, however, secretly opposed to the regime and aspires to its overthrow. Estranged from his wife, he embarks on an affair with one of his ministry colleagues, a woman named Julia. Recalling his life before the Party, Winston is drawn towards a resistance movement. But he is being set up and, having been exposed, is thrust into a process of 're-education' in which he is forced to confront his worst fear.

BRAVE NEW WORLD

Aldous Huxley published *Brave New World* in 1932. Like Orwell, he foresaw a nightmarish future but one that relied less on force and more on coercion. He wrote to Orwell in 1949:

I believe that the world's rulers will discover that infant conditioning and narco-hypnosis are more efficient, as instruments of government, than clubs and prisons, and that the lust for power can be just as completely satisfied by suggesting people into loving their servitude as by flogging and kicking them into obedience. In other words, I feel that the nightmare of *Nineteen Eighty-Four* is destined to modulate into the nightmare of a world having more resemblance to that which I imagined in *Brave New World*.

The book introduced an extraordinary number of terms that have since entered into common currency. Among them: Big Brother (the faceless dictator); doublethink (the acceptance of contrary ideas as a result of indoctrination); thoughtcrime (unorthodox thinking that is incompatible with official government lines); the Thought Police (the secret division of law enforcement that polices thoughtcrimes); Newspeak (language designed to conceal truth); and Room 101 (a torture chamber where a prisoner is confronted with their worst fear in a bid to break them). The notion that individuals ought to accept as truth whatever the Party decrees is summed up in the statement that Winston ponders in his diary: '2 + 2 = 5'. This sense of unstable truth is reflected in the names of the government ministries too: the Ministry of Truth that spreads lies, the Ministry of Peace that is concerned with war, the Ministry of Love where torture is practised, and the Ministry of Plenty, which contends with starvation. From the book's opening line ('It was a bright cold day in April, and the clocks were striking thirteen'), the sense of fluid reality and internal contradiction is palpable.

Orwell was one of the most politically engaged authors of his time. Born in 1903, he was a committed democratic socialist. His 1937 non-fiction work *The Road to Wigan Pier* examined the struggle of the British working-classes in light of the Great Depression, while the following year's *Homage to Catalonia* is an account of his experiences in the Spanish Civil War, during which he fought for the Republicans. He watched with increasing horror as Europe gave way to tyranny under both fascist and communist regimes. In 1945 he published a masterpiece of a novel, *Animal Farm*, that satirized the Stalinist USSR in a story about a group of farm animals that rise up against their farmer and set out to create their own model society. With swathes of the planet divided between the post-war superpowers, he then set about writing *Nineteen Eighty-Four*. It would become his last – and to many, greatest – novel. As he completed it on the Scottish island of Jura, he was dying of tuberculosis, succumbing in early 1950.

Nineteen Eighty-Four is an utterly compelling examination of how autocracies take root and how politics and, crucially, language can be corrupted and exploited. In an essay from 1946, 'Why I Write', he confirmed that his work since the mid-1930s had been 'written, directly or indirectly, against totalitarianism and for democratic socialism'. As well as having an incisive intellect and a prodigious imagination, Orwell was also a great stylist, which ensured his books won a mass audience. V. S. Pritchett praised *Nineteen Eighty-Four* in the *New Statesman*, writing: 'I do not think I have ever read a novel more frightening and depressing; and yet, such are the originality, the suspense, the speed of writing and withering indignation that it is impossible to put the book down.'

The novel fits into a lineage of related dystopian works, from Yevgeny Zamyatin's 1924 novel *We*, Arthur Koestler's *Darkness at Noon* and Karin Boye's *Kallocain* (both written in 1940) to later works like Ray Bradbury's *Fahrenheit 451* (1953), Margaret Atwood's *The Handmaid's Tale* (1985) and William Gibson's *Virtual Light* (1993). Each highly influential in their own right, none has come to surpass the enduring impact of Orwell. Even as the collapse of the Soviet empire in the early 1990s seemed to herald the ultimate victory of liberal democracy, *Nineteen Eighty-Four* has come to find new resonance for readers in the twenty-first century – an audience struggling to navigate a path through increasing surveillance, fake news, 'alternative facts', a new generation of 'strong men' leaders, and a social media environment in which oppositional groups choose their 'truth' and reject those who do not conform to it.

In 1949, Orwell wrote in *Ninety Eighty-Four*:

> Power is in tearing human minds to pieces and
> putting them together again in new shapes of
> your own choosing. Do you begin to see, then,
> what kind of world we are creating? It is the exact

opposite of the stupid hedonistic Utopias that
the old reformers imagined. A world of fear and
treachery is torment, a world of trampling and
being trampled upon, a world which will grow
not less but more merciless as it refines itself.

He would doubtless have been saddened by the continuing
relevance of his words.

TITLE: *THE SECOND SEX*

AUTHOR: SIMONE DE BEAUVOIR
DATE: 1949

. . . .

With *The Second Sex*, French philosopher and activist
Simone de Beauvoir wrote a keystone of Second Wave
feminism and arguably the single most impactful work of
feminism ever. In it, she laid out her thesis that women have
been historically trapped into a subservient role to men
and argued how they might break free of their shackles to
live more fulfilling lives.

As an existentialist, de Beauvoir believed that existence
is characterized by a fundamental 'nothingness' and that
it falls to the individual to create 'meaning' through the
choices that they make. In other words, each human life
lacks intrinsic value or merit at the cosmological level

and it is beholden upon the individual to give their own life value.

For women, de Beauvoir argued, this challenge has been made harder by the constraints imposed upon them by human society that has ascribed them a secondary role to men. It is an argument she built in the book's first volume, *Facts and Myths*, in which she cited countless historical examples to back up the claim. Man, she said, has traditionally been considered the default mode of 'Self', with Woman as 'the Other'.

Since prehistoric times, she set out to prove, Man has imposed his will on the world, defining himself through action. In contrast, Woman has been defined in opposition to Man, weak where Man is strong, inward-looking where Man strikes out into the world, and relying on Man's action to be 'saved'. This imposition of 'Otherness', she says, has not only ensured Woman's subjugation but has denied her fundamental humanity.

She sought to show how this sense of 'Otherness' had been created through various social discourses. Medicine, for instance, and disciplines such as psychoanalysis have traditionally considered women as 'the weaker sex', physiologically and mentally. History and literature, too, have reinforced notions of the dominant 'Man' and the secondary 'Woman', incapable of forging her own independent essence. Women, she suggests, have been trapped in the male-created myth of the 'eternal feminine', by which the feminine identity is tied to women's reproductive roles. While Woman as giver of life has been celebrated, her identity is also tied up with the inevitability of death that life brings, while her sexuality unnerves the patriarchy. The 'eternal feminine' has thus served to trap women in a socially constructed view of what it means to be a woman and has denied women the right to forge individual identities.

De Beauvoir also points out how, from a young age, girls are encouraged to become complicit in perpetuating this myth, conforming to a vague notion of femininity that forbids true realization of their own potential. As she memorably put it: 'One is not born, but rather becomes, a woman.' She is urged to embrace a 'maternal instinct' that, de Beauvoir says, is not innate, and is encouraged to imagine a future life as a support figure to a man, putting up with unfulfilling sexual relations and giving up on pursuing her own talents and ambitions – accepting the role of Other as Man seeks to realize his Self.

In volume two, *Lived Experience*, de Beauvoir describes how the traditional roles of women – wife, mother and also 'entertainer' – equate to 'holding away death but also refusing life'. Woman is left to be satisfied with mediocrity, compelling her towards complacency and passivity. De Beauvoir's suggested solution is to address the underpinning financial inequality between men and women. Women, she suggests, must undertake work that provides them with the financial wherewithal to support themselves and make possible a kind of liberation from the constraints of the 'eternal feminine' – a course that she recognizes is littered with obstacles. De Beauvoir also suggests that women should actively participate in more intellectual activities than tradition has allowed, transforming themselves from the 'objects' of tradition into the 'subjects' of their own lives.

The Second Sex is often seen as marking the transition from the First Wave of feminism (that which, broadly, sought to overturn obvious legally enshrined inequalities between the sexes such as unjust property and voting rights) to the Second Wave. This Second Wave, which went through to the 1980s, looked to debate wider issues of inequality in relation to, for example, the home, the work place, reproductive rights and sexual liberation. In de Beauvoir's own words: 'The free woman is just being born.'

The Second Sex was an instant phenomenon, selling tens of thousands of copies in its first weeks of release, and being translated into dozens of languages. It is difficult to imagine vital Second Wave works like Betty Friedan's *The Feminine Mystique*, Kate Millett's *Sexual Politics* or Germaine Greer's *The Female Eunuch* if de Beauvoir had not led the way. Inevitably, though, the work has not been without its critics. The Vatican was among those to ban it (the book deals in some detail with the question of a woman's right to abortion). But some feminist critics have also taken issue with aspects of the book, not least what some have suggested is de Beauvoir's underlying disappointment with women themselves – the suspicion that she thinks virtually all women have 'failed' in bringing meaning to their lives throughout history. But *The Second Sex* succeeded in reconfiguring the debate about women and feminism, compelling society to re-examine its expectations of womanhood and how each woman should be free to realize her full potential.

EXISTENTIALISM'S POWER COUPLE

It is one of those curious quirks of fate that de Beauvoir should so often find her name attached to that of a man – existentialist philosopher Jean-Paul Sartre, with whom she had a relationship from the late 1920s until his death in 1980. Theirs was not a traditional relationship, though. Both openly took other lovers (de Beauvoir was bisexual) and they never married, had children or lived together. It was an attempt at what de Beauvoir called 'authentic love' and she considered it the great success of her life. However, her diaries suggest that their partnership brought its own emotional strains. Not least, it raised the question of how painful even a mutually agreed infidelity can be?

TITLE: *CATCH–22*

AUTHOR: JOSEPH HELLER
DATE: 1961

. . . .

Catch–22 is a novel of comic satire with a dark underbelly. Set during the Second World War, it traces the frequently absurd and surreal experiences of US Air Force captain, John Yossarian – an anti-hero for the ages – and his companions. Published at the beginning of the 1960s at a time when US involvement was increasing in the Vietnam War, the book established itself not only as arguably the greatest anti-war novel of the century but also as a beacon of the nascent counter-culture. It signalled the coming of a new age in which the decision-making of authority was increasingly challenged and deference receded.

Heller was born in New York in 1923 and himself served in the Air Force during the Second World War as a bombardier on a B-52. A teacher and then an advertising copywriter, he only began to write about his wartime experiences, which included some sixty bombing raids, in the 1950s. It was one particular mission in August 1944, when Heller faced the real prospect of death as his aircraft flew over Avignon in France, that fundamentally shaped those attitudes to war that fuelled his most famous book. He was in part inspired to write it after reading *The Good Soldier Švejk*, an early example of an explicitly anti-war novel published in the 1920s by Czech author, Jaroslav Hašek.

Catch-22 is a study in how one may (or may not) hold on to one's individuality and humanity in the face of an all-powerful, impersonal military bureaucracy. In the very simplest terms, it is a novel about the madness of war. Told through a series of non-chronological and often tangential episodes incorporating the points of view of multiple characters, a sense of strangeness and dislocation permeates the text. Heller himself claimed that he wrote it with the Korean War, which raged in the 1950s, more prominent in his mind than the Second World War. Yossarian's challenge is to complete the necessary number of missions to secure his passage back home without losing his mind in the process.

'Catch-22' is a term that has now entered the popular lexicon to describe a particularly absurd, circular problem whose solution is denied by the terms of the problem itself.

For example, you need to fill out a form to order new ink for the printer, but you can't print the form because the printer has run out of ink.

MAKING THE TITLE COUNT

Catch-22 was never intended to have that title. Heller submitted the first chapter of the book to a magazine, which published it under the title of *Catch-18*. However, his agent asked for a retitling, fearing confusion with another novel published around the same time, *Mila 18* by Leon Uris. *Catch-11* was considered but was thought to be too close to the popular movie, *Ocean's 11*, while *Catch-17* was too close to *Stalag 17*. *Catch-14* was apparently rejected on the grounds that it was inherently not a funny enough number. So, it was *Catch-22*, with its sense of repetition and circularity, that eventually won the day.

Within the context of the novel, 'Catch-22' is never directly stated but is repeatedly referenced as proof of the ludicrous nature of the authorities' bureaucratic processes, trapping the characters in a Kafka-like nightmare. Most famously, it refers to a condition that allows for crew of unfit mind to be excused from flying missions. All one had to do was to apply to be excused. But as Yossarian states, the act of having concern for your safety in the face of the real and immediate dangers the flying crew faced indicated a rational mind at work. By the very action of applying, the applicant demonstrated their sanity and so would be refused. In blunt terms, you had to be crazy to want to fly and sane not to want to, but if you were sane you had to fly.

As the book progresses, the full horror of the characters' experiences come to light. Yossarian comes to regard his own commanding officers as being as much a threat to him as the enemy. The novel riffs on all manner of themes, from the dangers of unfettered capitalism (as epitomized by the 'Syndicate' run by the Base's amoral entrepreneur, Milo Minderbinder) to the nature of God (Yossarian describes the God that he doesn't believe in as a 'colossal, immortal blunderer').

When the book first came out, many critics did not know what to make of it. The *New Yorker*, for example, noted that it 'doesn't even seem to be written; instead, it gives the impression of having been shouted onto paper'. The *New York Times* said it was 'not even a good novel' but nonetheless qualified the statement by claiming it was 'wildly original, brilliantly comic, brutally gruesome … a dazzling performance'.

Even as the critics fumbled to assess it, the book began to garner a cult following, especially among the young. It chimed perfectly with the anti-authoritarian vibe of the time and took hold in the popular imagination as the anti-Vietnam War movement gathered pace. While *Catch-22*'s anti-war message is indeed potent, it also speaks more broadly of the human condition but in a way that allows readers to laugh out loud. A triumph of both form and content, it won no major literary awards but within a few years was established as a modern classic. Years later, Heller would say that when, as frequently happened, some critic or another pointed out that he'd never done anything as good as *Catch-22*, he was tempted to reply, 'Who *has*?'

At once comically playful, horrific and tragic, *Catch-22* is a book that hit its moment in history, holding up a mirror to a world that found its reflection unflattering. A world where war is industrialized, commerce conquers all and individuals find themselves as unwitting collateral damage. A world that felt itself going slowly mad, caught up in unbreakable cycles of self-destruction. It was always much more than just another war novel. Heller himself said that he was less interested in writing about war than in examining 'the personal relationships in bureaucratic authority'. We all instinctively understand how it feels to be caught in a catch-22 but it fell to Heller to give voice to it. 'Everyone in my book accuses everyone else of being crazy,' he once said. 'Frankly, I think the whole society is nuts – and the question is: What does a sane man do in an insane society?'

TITLE: *SILENT SPRING*

AUTHOR: RACHEL CARSON

DATE: 1962

. . . .

Silent Spring was written by Rachel Carson, a US marine biologist who had become convinced that the then rapidly expanding use of pesticides was having a seriously detrimental effect on the environment. The chemical industry, which she suggested was misrepresenting the impact of its products to the public, fought back fiercely but Carson's arguments proved highly persuasive to a receptive American audience.

The book prompted a reversal in national policy with regard to pesticide use and was a major influencing factor in the establishment of the US Environmental Protection Agency. But of still greater significance was its role in raising awareness of broader environmental issues among a public that had previously been largely unengaged with the subject. As such, the work is widely considered the world's first major work of environmentalist literature and a pivotal moment in the growth of the international environmental movement.

Born in 1907 in Pennsylvania, Carson was educated at the Woods Hole Marine Biological Laboratory and then Johns Hopkins University in Baltimore. She was that rare combination of talented scientist and skilled communicator, a professional aquatic biologist who wrote and edited for a number of publications, eventually becoming editor-in-chief for the US Fish and Wildlife Service. Then, in 1951, she wrote *The Sea Around Us*, which became a bestseller and earned her a US National Book Award. Flushed with this success, she was now able to devote herself full-time to writing.

THE FIRST LETTER

One of the factors that persuaded Carson to write her book was a letter written to the *Boston Herald* in January 1958 by her friend, Olga Owens Huckins. Huckins reported the death of birds on her property in Duxbury, Massachusetts, following the spraying of DDT there to get rid of mosquitoes. After a pilot dumped a small excess of the chemical on her land, she reported: 'The "harmless" shower-bath killed seven of our lovely songbirds outright. We picked up three dead bodies the next morning right by the door. They were birds that had lived close to us, trusted us, and built their nests in our trees year after year.' Sending a copy of the note to Carson, Huckins perhaps inadvertently helped alter the course of environmental history, and those birds at least might not have died in vain.

Meanwhile, American agriculture was becoming increasingly reliant on a 'miracle' pesticide called DDT. It had been developed shortly before the outbreak of the Second World War and had come to wider notice when it was used in the South Pacific to reduce the populations of malaria-carrying insects on islands hosting US troops. DDT was then quickly developed for civilian use, coming onto the market in 1945. Its great selling-point was that, unlike other pesticides, it did not target a small range of species but could erase huge numbers at a stroke. The chemical industry highlighted the great advantages that this could bring to farmers and there were few dissenting voices. Its inventor, Paul Hermann Müller, even received a Nobel Prize in 1948 'for his discovery of the high efficiency of DDT as a contact poison against several arthropods'.

However, it became increasingly apparent that the indiscriminate nature of such chemicals had serious implications. When the Department of Agriculture began aerial spraying of DDT in 1957 to eradicate fire ants, Carson was among several interested parties keeping an eye on its impact. This was the beginning of what would become *Silent Spring*, for which she secured a publishing deal in 1958. However, it soon became clear that such was the quantity of data and other evidence she was gathering that the book would be greater in scope than she first imagined.

By 1960, she'd looked at several hundred instances of pesticide exposure, examining the impact on humans (including potential carcinogenic effects and genetic changes) and on the wider environment too. She spent the majority of the following year completing the manuscript, a task made harder as she also faced a diagnosis of breast cancer.

She urged that pesticide sprays should be restricted as much as possible, focusing on a biotic approach ahead of chemical pesticides. She warned that ecosystems were being endangered by the non-selective nature of pesticides that were wiping out essential species. Entire food chains were being poisoned out of existence, from the insects up. DDT stayed active in ecosystems for weeks and months at a time, even after dilution by rainwater. Moreover, she raised the prospect that some pests – for instance, malaria-carrying mosquitoes – might develop resistance.

Highlighting the damage that humans are capable of inflicting on the world, Carson thought about calling the book *Man Against Nature*. Instead, she opted for the title that she had until then reserved for a chapter on birds. It was, the story goes, inspired by lines from John Keats' 'La Belle Dame sans Merci': 'The sedge is wither'd from the lake, And no birds sing.' The book was serialized in the *New Yorker* prior to publication and received significant public attention, but the chemical industry, fearful of its revelations, came out strongly against it and Carson.

There were unsuccessful attempts to sue her, her publisher and the *New Yorker* for libel. An expensive PR campaign was launched that promoted the benefits of pesticide use while seeking to discredit Carson personally, often in pretty crude ways. One former US secretary of agriculture questioned in public 'why a spinster with no children was so interested in genetics'. The American Cyanamid Company, meanwhile, claimed: 'If Man were to faithfully follow the teachings of Miss Carson, we would return to the Dark Ages, and the insects and diseases and vermin would once again inherit the earth.'

But the public's concern had been mobilized in an unprecedented way, and only more so when CBS ran a television special in the spring of 1963 based around the book. 'Man's attitude toward nature,' Carson told the documentary-makers, 'is today critically important simply because we have now acquired a fateful power to alter and destroy nature. But Man is a part of nature, and his war against nature is inevitably a war against himself.'

Carson tragically died as a result of her cancer in April 1964. By then, the book had sold in excess of a million copies. Moreover, it would inspire genuine change. President Kennedy had ordered the President's Science

Advisory Committee to examine the claims made in *Silent Spring*, as a result of which a nationwide ban was implemented on DDT in agriculture. Carson had also highlighted the conflict of interest that existed as a result of the Department of Agriculture being responsible for both representing the interests of the agricultural industry and regulating pesticides. So, in 1970, the US Environmental Protection Agency was established.

But most importantly, *Silent Spring* changed the terms of the environmental debate and spurred the growth of a populist environmental movement, both in the US and abroad. By highlighting the threats to human health and to the existence of entire animal species – while also warning of the questionable integrity of industry – she tapped into a discourse that engaged the public at large. H. Patricia Hynes, retired Professor of Environmental Health at the Boston University School of Public Health, has noted: '*Silent Spring* altered the balance of power in the world. No one since would be able to sell pollution as the necessary underside of progress so easily or uncritically.' Renowned broadcaster and naturalist David Attenborough, meanwhile, has suggested that – with the exception of Darwin's *Origin of Species* – *Silent Spring* is the book that changed the scientific world more than any other.

TITLE: *WHY WE CAN'T WAIT*

AUTHOR: MARTIN LUTHER KING JR
DATE: 1964

. . . .

Why We Can't Wait tells the story of Martin Luther King's non-violent civil rights movement and its campaign against racial segregation, especially in Birmingham, Alabama, in 1963. As well as being a stunning historical document recording the civil rights movement at a pivotal moment in its history – at the start of what its author calls the 'Negro Revolution' – it is also a call to arms that continues to resonate in a world still divided along racial lines.

Martin Luther King Jr, born in Atlanta, Georgia, in 1929, was a Baptist minister who had come to national attention as a civil rights leader by the mid-1950s, fuelled by his Christian faith and his admiration for pioneers of non-violent protest such as Mahatma Gandhi. In 1955, he was prominent in the Montgomery bus protest, prompted by the arrest of Rosa Parks for refusing to give up her seat to a white passenger as the law demanded. King subsequently became president of the Southern Christian Leadership Conference (SCLC).

Against stiff competition, Birmingham, Alabama, was considered to be among the most racially segregated of all American cities in the early 1960s. King and the SCLC became involved in protests aimed at forcing the hand of employers to take on workers regardless of their race. The campaign also sought an end to segregation in public spaces, and was conducted on the principles of mass action (e.g. marches and protests) and non-violence.

The campaign's demands were largely ignored by the Birmingham authorities and its business leaders. However, tensions escalated and one protest-walk, undertaken in groups of fifty moving from one of the city's Baptist churches to City Hall, resulted in thousands of arrests. Then Commissioner of Public Safety, Eugene 'Bull' Connor, authorized the use of high-pressure hoses and police attack dogs on protestors, with many children and bystanders also caught up in the clashes.

King was among those to end up in a prison cell in April 1963. Amid criticism of the campaign from some local religious leaders, he composed 'Letter from Birmingham Jail', which was widely circulated and brought the campaign national and international attention. It was from this letter that *Why We Can't Wait* evolved, documenting the struggles of the civil rights campaign in the American South that spring and summer. While he watched Asia and Africa 'moving with jet-like speed toward gaining political independence', King was frustrated by the US's 'horse-and-buggy pace'.

I HAVE A DREAM

Just three months after the conclusion of the Birmingham campaign, King was a pivotal figure in the March on Washington, held on 28 August 1963, to demand greater civil rights. One of the largest rallies in the nation's history, it attracted some quarter of a million protestors. It was here, in front of the Lincoln Memorial, that King delivered his iconic 'I have a dream' speech. A poll in 1999 of 137 leading scholars of public address ranked it the best political speech of the twentieth century.

Why We Can't Wait – which King prepared in co-operation with several other prominent civil rights figures including Stanley Levison, Clarence Jones and Bayard Rustin – was a rallying call. 'For years now, I have heard the word "Wait!" It rings in the ear of every Negro with piercing familiarity,' wrote King. 'This "Wait" has almost always meant "Never".

We must come to see, with one of our distinguished jurists, that "justice too long delayed is justice denied".'

The book seeks to put the Birmingham campaign into some historical context, and to explain why the 'Negro Revolution' had seemed to some observers to explode out of nowhere. King promised to those bewildered by recent events that there would be more to come. He suggested that the campaign had struck like lightning with 'frightening intensity' but stemmed from three centuries of abuse, humiliation and deprivation that could not 'find voice in a whisper'. Birmingham under the yoke of 'Bull' Connor was, he said, reminiscent of a city in the era of slavery, where the black population was denied basic human rights and faced intimidation and violence if they complained.

He also cited the slow pace of reform following the landmark *Brown* v *Board of Education* ruling of 1954 that found segregation in public schools unconstitutional. A general lack of confidence in the political establishment and the ongoing impact of the Great Depression that hit America's black population particularly harshly were further drivers for protest. He was, he noted, writing exactly a hundred years on from Abraham Lincoln's Emancipation Proclamation and yet millions remained oppressed.

King advocated the ongoing use of non-violent methods – what he described as 'the need for mankind to overcome oppression and violence without resorting to violence and oppression'. He recognized that in Birmingham, being arrested had itself become a political act, weakening its strength as a tool of oppression. As the jails filled with prisoners united in a common cause, the sheer weight of their number proved a problem for the authorities and allowed the protestors to draw still greater public attention to their demands.

King likened the Birmingham campaign to the Battle of Bunker Hill – referencing the American War of Independence encounter in which the American forces began to seriously mobilize against their oppressor. But, he warned, the campaign in Alabama should not breed over-confidence or complacency. It was rather to be seen as the first step on a long road. He called for a bill of rights that, among other things, would look to compensate the disadvantaged for historically unpaid wages. He also sought to ally his supporters alongside poor whites and other oppressed groups. The success of such a coalition, he hoped, might ultimately foster non-violence everywhere and usher in world peace.

Such a utopian vision is yet to come to pass, but the Birmingham campaign and *Why We Can't Wait* did spur change, not least the passage of the 1964 Civil Rights Act that outlawed many forms of racial discrimination. Within Birmingham itself, the city authorities agreed to a process of desegregation. But the deal led the Klu Klux Klan to bomb King's hotel room and, just five years later, he would be shot dead by an assassin in Memphis, Tennessee. *Why We Can't Wait* stands as a testament to one of the giant figures of twentieth-century geopolitics, serving as a testament of hope even as the work that King began remains to be completed.

In 2006, Barack Obama – then primed to become the

first person of colour to serve as America's president – paid tribute to a figure without whom his own ascent would have been impossible. 'Through words,' Obama said, 'he gave voice to the voiceless. Through deeds he gave courage to the faint of heart. By dint of vision, and determination, and most of all faith in the redeeming power of love, he endured the humiliation of arrest, the loneliness of a prison cell, the constant threats to his life, until he finally inspired a nation to transform itself, and begin to live up to the meaning of its creed.'

TITLE: *A BRIEF HISTORY OF TIME*

AUTHOR: STEPHEN HAWKING
DATE: 1988

. . . .

One of the bestselling science books of all time, *A Brief History of Time* helped change the popular understanding of cosmology (the science of the origin and development of the universe) and theoretical physics, introducing the intricacies of, for example, quantum mechanics and imaginary time to a global, lay audience. 'I am pleased a book on science competes with the memoirs of pop stars,' Hawking would later note. 'Maybe there is some hope for the human race.'

Hawking was born in Oxford, England, in 1942, and showed early academic promise, winning a place to study

Physics at University College, Oxford. After graduating with a First, he then studied for a PhD at Trinity Hall, Cambridge. It was in this period that he received the devastating diagnosis that he was suffering from amyotrophic lateral sclerosis (ALS, for short) – an early-onset slow-progressing form of motor neurone disease, which over the subsequent decades would leave him paralysed and unable to speak unaided.

BETTER THAN SEX

If *A Brief History of Time* was the stand-out science publishing sensation of the late twentieth century, its counterpart in popular culture came in 1992 when Madonna published her controversial 'coffee-table book', *Sex*. With its adult content, the book sold extravagantly in its early days, quickly notching sales of 1.5 million. But it never came close to the estimated 25 million that Hawking's book sold. Talking of *A Brief History* in 2004, former Microsoft Chief Technology Officer, Nathan Myhrvold, wryly noted: 'It outsold Madonna's book *Sex*, and by a huge margin, and who would have predicted that?'

But Hawking refused to let the news of his illness slow him down. In fact, faced with premature death, he grasped every opportunity with a fervour and passion that had not hitherto always been apparent. He embarked on a slew of ground-breaking work in the area of cosmology, and black holes especially, forging a particularly close association with mathematical physicist Roger Penrose. Together, they investigated black holes within the framework of general relativity, predicting that they send out radiation. (Penrose would eventually be awarded the Nobel Prize for Physics – one of the few accolades that eluded Hawking.)

While Hawking was a shining light in the scientific firmament by the mid-1980s, he was hardly the household name that he was destined to become. He was conjuring with the idea of a 'theory of everything' that brought together general relativity and quantum mechanics into a cohesive whole – and he also started to mull over the idea of a popular science book. His idea was to write a book about the origins of the universe that would explain the great leaps made in our collective knowledge over the previous few decades, but that would be written in language that anyone could grasp. A very tall order. He was determined, for instance, to avoid reams of complex equations and, in the end, he included just one – arguably the most famous equation in history, Einstein's $E=mc^2$. It is said he kept the number so low because he had been told each additional equation would halve his readership.

Hawking got himself a hotshot New York agent and sought out the biggest book deal he could find. He signed up with Bantam in 1984, a firm with mass-market heft that offered a quarter of a million dollars for US rights alone.

Hawking's health took a downturn the following year and the writing process was arduous but the book was ready to roll off the press in 1988. But not before his editor, Peter Guzzardi, made the inspired decision to rename the book. Instead of Hawking's planned: *From the Big Bang to Black Holes: A Short History of Time* it now became *A Brief History of Time: From the Big Bang to Black Holes*. An introduction by another of the century's scientific giants, Carl Sagan, helped to create a real buzz around the launch.

At the core of the book was Hawking's conviction that science would soon hit upon the ultimate theory of how our universe came into being. Famously, he likened this achievement to knowing 'the mind of God'. The sales that followed were unprecedented for a science book – it achieved 147 weeks on the *New York Times* bestseller list in the US and 237 weeks in the *Times'* bestsellers in the UK, not to mention translation into over forty languages. ('I knew it was going to be a success when it was translated into Serbo-Croatian,' Hawking once quipped.) Jokes began to circulate about it being the bestselling book that people didn't read beyond Chapter 1. Critics pointed out that the prose was not always unfailingly elegant and some of the science was very difficult to grasp. But Hawking did succeed in introducing millions to such concepts as the Big Bang and imaginary time (the idea that was, he acknowledged, 'the thing in the book with which people have most trouble'). Maybe not everyone could digest it, but it surely served as an inspiration to a great many aspiring scientists across the planet.

Confined to a wheelchair and able to speak only with an electronic voice box with a highly idiosyncratic tone, Hawking became the most famous scientist on the planet. Only the wild-haired Albert Einstein has ever enjoyed a comparable level of celebrity among scientists. For the rest of his life, until his death in 2018 – exceeding by decades his doctors' life-expectancy prognosis – he was a major public figure and educator as well as cutting-edge researcher. Where Hawking fits in the pantheon of great scientists is a subject of some debate. It can be argued he was not responsible for a scientific revolution in the mode of a Newton or an Einstein. But in terms of communicating complex science to the masses, *A Brief History of Time* stands alongside the great works of scientific writing – a literary Big Bang.

Martin Rees – a cosmologist, astrophysicist, Astronomer Royal and President of the Royal Society – would say of Hawking in 2015: 'His name will live in the annals of science; millions have had their cosmic horizons widened by his bestselling books; and even more, around the world, have been inspired by a unique example of achievement against all the odds – a manifestation of astonishing willpower and determination.'

TITLE: *LONG WALK TO FREEDOM*

AUTHOR: NELSON MANDELA

DATE: 1994

. . . .

Long Walk to Freedom is the memoir of Nelson Mandela, the central figure in black South Africa's fight to dismantle the country's apartheid regime – a system of government that privileged the rights of the white minority over those of the black majority. Jailed for his political activities for twenty-seven years, Mandela was freed in 1990 and four years later was elected president in the nation's first post-apartheid elections. He emerged as an international icon and a unifying force for good. As South African Nobel Laureate Nadine Gardiner would note: 'He is at the epicentre of our time, ours in South Africa, and yours, wherever you are.' *Long Walk to Freedom* was a landmark work that documented not only Mandela's personal journey, but his country's extraordinary social and political transition too.

Written in collaboration with American author and editor, Richard Stengel, the book covers the full expanse of

Mandela's life, from his birth in a village in Cape Province into the royal family of the Xhosa-speaking Thembu people. He was raised, he noted, with the name Rolihlahla, a moniker sometimes given to playfully suggest a 'trouble-maker'. In later life, though, he would be known by his clan name, Madiba.

Mandela described an adolescence and education in which he felt himself to be at once privileged in comparison with much of the black population but acutely aware of the secondary position in which the European-rooted authorities held black culture. After studying at the University of Fort Hare – a tertiary institute for black students where he met future confederates, including Oliver Tambo – he made his way to Johannesburg, in part to escape the threat of an arranged marriage. There he began a legal career as well as exploring his sympathies with communism and nurturing his association with the African National Congress (ANC), the political party that would become the country's most potent opposition to the apartheid system formally introduced in the late 1940s.

Although initially committed to peaceful protest and civil disobedience, in the face of the increasing violence of the apartheid regime – as epitomized by the Sharpeville Massacre, when sixty-nine protestors were killed at a police station while protesting against the so-called pass laws that required blacks to carry identity papers – he concluded that the battle against apartheid would require the adoption of guerrilla tactics. In 1963–4 he was a defendant in the so-called Rivonia Trial on charges connected to acts of sabotage and their commission. Found guilty, he received a life sentence, but he also entered the international consciousness with an address from the dock in which he said:

> During my lifetime I have dedicated my
> life to this struggle of the African people. I
> have fought against white domination, and I
> have fought against black domination. I have
> cherished the ideal of a democratic and free
> society in which all persons will live together
> in harmony and with equal opportunities. It
> is an ideal for which I hope to live for and to
> see realized. But, my Lord, if it needs to be, it
> is an ideal for which I am prepared to die.

POSTHUMOUS SEQUEL

It was always Mandela's intention to write a further memoir dealing with his time as president, but such a book never emerged in his lifetime. However, in 2017, celebrated South African writer Mandla Langa used Mandela's unfinished manuscript along with archive material and interviews to complete the volume, which was published as *Dare Not Linger: The Presidential Years* – a title referencing the final line of the previous volume. It also included a prologue by Mandela's third wife, Graça Machel, herself a noted humanitarian and a former wife of Samora Machel, President of Mozambique from 1975 until 1986.

During his almost three decades of incarceration, most notoriously on Robben Island, international pressure ramped up against the apartheid regime until Mandela was finally released during the tenure of President F. W. de Klerk. Mandela's magnanimity in the face of his many struggles gave him a moral authority arguably unrivalled by any other living person, and the path was set for the dismantling of the apartheid system and the establishment of democratic elections in 1994 – an election that resulted in Mandela serving a single term as president before withdrawing from front-line politics, while remaining a major public figure both at home and abroad.

Long Walk to Freedom was a significant component in cementing his reputation and fleshing out his philosophy of compassion, empathy and compromise. Mandela's charisma not only attracted fellow world leaders and public figures who yearned to be photographed alongside him but appealed to ordinary people the world over otherwise immune to the draw of politicians. In his autobiography, he devoted time to exploring some of the credos by which he lived – such that the greatest glory lies not in never falling, but in rising every time one falls, and that if people can learn to hate, they can also be taught to love. His wisdom proved to have universal appeal in an age when it was not always in great supply on the international stage.

Mandela concluded the book – which sold 15 million copies and spawned a successful Hollywood movie – by observing that he could not rest for a moment, for with freedom comes responsibilities, and he dared not linger because his long walk was not yet ended. Indeed, he had almost two decades longer until his death in late 2013. Born into tribal royalty, imprisoned as a terrorist and then lauded as a quasi-saint, he documents in *Long Walk to Freedom* one of the most extraordinary life stories of modern times, a contemporary *Odyssey*. Mandela's unrivalled legacy, both personal and political, was encapsulated in a eulogy given at his funeral by Barack Obama:

Mandela taught us the power of action, but he also taught us the power of ideas; the importance of reason and arguments; the need to study not only those who you agree with, but also those who you don't agree with. And when the night grows dark, when injustice weighs heavy on our hearts, when our best-laid plans seem beyond our reach, let us think of Madiba and the words that brought him comfort within the four walls of his cell: "It matters not how strait the gate, how charged with punishments the scroll, I am the master of my fate: I am the captain of my soul."

AFTERWORD

It has frequently been claimed that the book is on its last legs. In a world of instant gratification, where the internet and streaming services vie for our attention, and where 30-second videos and 280 characters are the preferred mediums of communication, the book is regularly dismissed as a relic of the past. But, to paraphrase Mark Twain, rumours of its demise have been greatly exaggerated.

Until Gutenberg introduced his printing press around the middle of the fifteenth century, the number of manuscript books in Europe's libraries numbered no more than a few tens of thousands. Now, some three hundred thousand titles are commercially published each year in the US alone – a figure bolstered by millions more self-published titles. We are awash with books.

It is true that they face stiff competition from other forms of media like never before, and that the sheer volume of published works does not necessarily make it easy for the literary cream to rise to the top. Nonetheless, it is clear that the book still plays an integral role in our shared culture. Over several thousand years, it has proved itself an extraordinarily durable format that evolves as the world changes.

To this day, there is nothing quite like it for exploring a subject in real depth. To read a book is a commitment of time and energy – both intellectual and emotional. It is a chance to engage with consciences that you would never otherwise encounter. René Descartes characterized reading books as like having conversations with the finest minds of the past. The effort required to read a text is more than matched by the rewards it brings – the chance to enter different realms from the ones we inhabit in the day to day. An opportunity to connect.

This volume represents a smorgasbord of just a few of the most significant and remarkable works from throughout history – books that help tell the story of our civilization. I hope you have enjoyed this short literary voyage through time and that it might inspire your own, new journeys. As you set sail again, keep in mind the words of the nineteenth-century American academic, Charles W. Eliot: 'Books are the quietest and most constant of friends; they are the most accessible and wisest of counsellors, and the most patient of teachers.'

Select Bibliography

Bannock, Graham and Baxter, R. E., *The Penguin Dictionary of Economics* (Penguin, 2011)

Barański, Zygmunt G. and Gilson, Simon (eds), *The Cambridge Companion to Dante's 'Commedia'* (Cambridge University Press, 2018)

Blackburn, Simon, *The Oxford Dictionary of Philosophy* (Oxford University Press, 2016)

Bowker, John (ed.), *The Oxford Dictionary of World Religions* (Oxford University Press, 1997)

Buck, Claire, *Women's Literature A–Z* (Bloomsbury, 1994)

Clark, Timothy, *The Cambridge Introduction to Literature and the Environment* (Cambridge University Press, 2011)

Dalley, Stephanie (ed.), *Myths from Mesopotamia: Creation, the Flood, Gilgamesh, and Others* (Oxford University Press, 2000)

De Grazia, Margreta and Wells, Stanley, *The New Cambridge Companion to Shakespeare* (Cambridge University Press, 2010)

Denisoff, Dennis and Schaffer, Talia (eds), *The Routledge Companion to Victorian Literature* (Routledge, 2019)

D'haen, Theo, Damrosch, David and Kadir, Djelal (eds), *The Routledge Companion to World Literature* (Routledge, 2011)

Egginton, William, *The Man Who Invented Fiction: How Cervantes Ushered in the Modern World* (Bloomsbury, 2016)

Emerson, Caryl, *The Cambridge Introduction to Russian Literature* (Cambridge University Press, 2011)

Gribbin, John, *The Scientists: A History of Science Told Through the Lives of Its Greatest Inventors* (Random House, 2004)

Gutzwiller, Kathryn, *Guide to Hellenistic Literature* (John Wiley & Sons, 2007)

Hsia, Chih-tsing, *The Classic Chinese Novel: A Critical Introduction* (Columbia University Press, 1968)

Kemp, Peter (ed.), *The Oxford Dictionary of Literary Quotations* (Oxford University Press, 1997)

Kupperman Joel, *Classic Asian Philosophy: A Guide to the Essential Texts* (Oxford University Press, 2006)

Marcus, Marvin, *Japanese Literature: From Murasaki to Murakami* (Association for Asian Studies, 2021)

Treharne, Elaine, *Medieval Literature: A Very Short Introduction* (Oxford University Press, 2015)

Walder, Dennis, *Literature in the Modern World: Critical Essays and Documents* (Oxford University Press, 1991)

Wellbery, David E. *et al.*, *A New History of German Literature* (Harvard University Press, 2005)

INDEX